Jewelry

—IN A JIFFY—

Jewelry
—IN A JIFFY—

Fransie Snyman

FIREFLY BOOKS

A FIREFLY BOOK

Published by Firefly Books Ltd. 2011

Copyright © Metz Press 2011
Text Copyright © 2011 Fransie Snyman
Photographs Copyright © 2011 Metz Press

First Printing

Publisher Cataloging-in-Publication Data (U.S.)
Snyman, Fransie.
Jewelry in a jiffy : more than 55 quick and easy bead projects
/ Fransie Snyman
[144] p. : col. photos. ;   cm.
Summary: A guide to making fashionable, personalized beaded
jewelry, including creative projects, clear explanations of basic
skills, and instructional color photographs.
ISBN-13: 978-1-55407–936-0 (pbk.)
1. Beadwork. 2. Jewelry making. I. Title.
745.5942 dc22   TT860.S696 2011

Library and Archives Canada Cataloguing in Publication
Snyman, Fransie
Jewelry in a jiffy : more than 55 quick and easy bead
projects / Fransie Snyman.
ISBN-13: 978-1-55407-936-0
1. Beadwork. 2. Jewelry making. I. Title.
TT860.S69 2011   745.58'2   C2011-903392-5

Published in the United States by
Firefly Books (U.S.) Inc.
P.O. Box 1338, Ellicott Station
Buffalo, New York 14205

Published in Canada by
Firefly Books Ltd.
66 Leek Crescent
Richmond Hill, Ontario L4B 1H1

Printed in China

Editor: Wilsa Metz
Translator: Louise Vorster
Design and layout: Angie Hausner
Photographer: Ivan Naudé

Contents

Introduction

There is no better therapy than being creative! Producing something original, and being able to admire the outcome, is an extremely satisfying experience. I have tried my hand at numerous creative activities, and beadwork has to be one of the most addictive. The variety of beads on the market is staggering, and continues to grow by the day.

One of the best aspects of beadwork is that you can buy beads to suit your budget. Plastic beads are cheap and can be used for costume jewelry that will most likely be worn for one season only. Glass beads are more expensive, but the finished product is also much more durable. Resin — a special kind of plastic — is increasingly being used in the manufacturing of beads. It is wonderful to be able to work with Swarovski or other crystals to create lasting products that could well become heirlooms.

I am normally fairly patient, but when it comes to art or craftwork, I want to see rapid results. As the working mother of a large family, my time is limited. Therefore all the projects in this book are really quick and easy to make – no intricate weaving techniques or patterns to follow! With three daughters in the house, I often get a request to "quickly" make something for a specific occasion.

Although the designs in this book take little time to complete, for most of them careful planning is of the essence.

"The more haste, the less speed," the saying goes, so do not leap into a project head over heels. Thorough planning will save you from having to start a particular project all over again, thus wasting unnecessary time.

Each project is described step by step, but the real challenge is for you to apply the ideas and use your own creativity to produce unique pieces. You can quite easily use different color combinations or find similar beads to create your own personal variation of a design. Alternative ideas are given for most projects.

As this is principally a book of ideas, the section on findings, techniques and equipment focuses exclusively on the basics. Only the techniques used in this book are explained, and only the most basic requirements and equipment discussed.

Enjoy — and remember that craftwork should always be a pleasurable experience for the maker!

Note on measurements: As bead measurements are typically expressed in millimeters, metric measurements (mm, cm, m) have been used throughout this book. The following conversions may help you in translating these to inches or feet, if required.

1 mm = approx 1/32 inches   1 inch = 2.5 cm

1 cm = 3/8 inches   1 foot = 30 cm

1 m = 3 feet 3 inches

Basic techniques

Only techniques used in this book are explained here. I have no doubt that some of you will prefer to use your own methods, but these are the ones I have found the easiest. Remember that beadwork should always be an enjoyable experience — therefore choose the method you are comfortable with.

The following are the techniques that most often occur in the projects:

Making an eyelet

Eyelets are mainly used for linking beads together or for connecting beads to a chain.

Making eyelets can be quite frustrating initially, but with a little bit of practice you will soon master the technique. You may notice that my method is somewhat different from the method used in most books. However, this is the method that works best for me.

Thread the bead or beads onto a headpin, then bend the pin to form a 90° angle with respect to the bead.

Using your round-nose pliers, form an eyelet around the nose of the pliers. The closer to the tip, the smaller the eyelet will be.

Once you are happy with the size and shape of the eyelet, cut the excess wire right up against the eyelet using wire cutters.

Neatly flatten the eyelet using flat-nose pliers.

Make sure that the two ends meet tightly so that whatever is connected to the eyelet will not slip out.

Using a shell end with a crimp bead

Thread the stringing material through the hole in the shell end.

Thread a crimp bead onto the string.

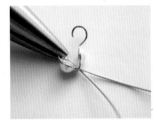

Thread the string back over the crimp bead and through the hole in the shell end.

Firmly close the crimp bead.

Close the shell end.

Connect a fastener or ring to the shell end, then tightly bend the eyelet closed.

Finishing a string with a knot

Beads that are strung on elastic are usually finished off with a knot. The knot should be very secure to prevent it from becoming undone, causing the beads to fall off and get lost.

Wrapping the left end of the elastic over the right end, pull it through downward.

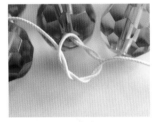

Wrap the right end over the left, pulling it through the loop twice.

Pull the knot tight...

...and apply a drop of glue to the knot. Allow the glue to dry completely, then trim the excess elastic close to the knot.

Pull the knot into the hole of an adjacent bead.

Attaching a fastener with cord

A quick and easy way to attach a fastener to cord is by simply knotting it.

Doubling up the cord or string, thread it through the fastener ring.

Thread the two loose ends through the loop, then pull the knot tight.

Opening and closing a jump ring

When a jump ring is opened and closed, care must be taken to prevent the shape from being distorted.

Using flat-nose pliers, hold the ring tightly. Open the ring by bending one end to the front and the other to the back.

Insert whatever is needed into the ring, then bend the ring closed again.

Attaching cord or thongs to a cord crimp end

Insert all the cord or thong ends into the flat part of the crimp end.

Apply a drop of glue to the cords to ensure that all the ends remain secure inside the crimp end.

Start by folding one side of the crimp end over.

Making sure that all the cord ends are still in place, fold the remaining side of the crimp end over, then close firmly to secure.

Findings, fasteners and tools

Apart from beads, findings such as headpins, eyepins and spacers are used in beadwork. These components can be functional or decorative. Although they may seem an insignificant part of beadwork, it is important to choose good-quality materials. Cheap findings of inferior quality can reduce the value of your pieces, while good-quality findings will add to their charm. The use of findings also plays an important role in the appearance of jewelry, turning a plain and ordinary piece into something original and unique.

Only the findings used in this book are discussed here. There are many more available, but that could take up a book of its own! Pay a regular visit to your local bead store — new findings appear on the market continually.

1 Headpins

Headpins are very similar in appearance to long dressmaker's pins. They have flat ends which prevent them from passing through bead holes and are available in various lengths, thicknesses and colors. Headpins are most often used for making earrings and for connecting beads to chains or jump rings. The smaller the beads you are working with, the thinner the headpins to be used. If the beads you use have large holes, a spacer or seed bead can be threaded onto the headpin before the bead to prevent the headpin from passing through the bead hole.

2 Decorative headpins

These are used mainly for earrings, but can be very effective where beads are connected to chains.

3 Eyepins

Instead of a blunt tip, eyepins end in an eyelet. They, too, come in a variety of lengths, thicknesses and colors, and are used where longer bead chains need to be linked. Eyepins can also be used instead of headpins if you are working with large-holed beads.

4 Shell ends

Shell ends are used at the ends of bead strings to finish them off and to attach the fasteners. They are available in different sizes and colors.

5 Bead caps

Bead caps can have a dramatic influence on the appearance of a piece of jewelry, providing a very special finish to the piece. I never realized their value until I started using them myself. Like all other findings, bead caps come in many different kinds and colors — from minute to very large, and from rough to the finest filigree.

6 Spacers

Spacers are small beads that are used for separating larger beads. They can also be employed as focal points between beads. Usually made of metal, they come in a huge variety of sizes and colors.

7 Multistrand spacers

Multistrand spacers usually comprise thin bars with multiple holes for separating multiple strands of beads. Usually made of metal, they also come in wood, shell, bone and plastic. Some are very decorative, while others are plain and merely functional.

1 2

3 4

5 7 6

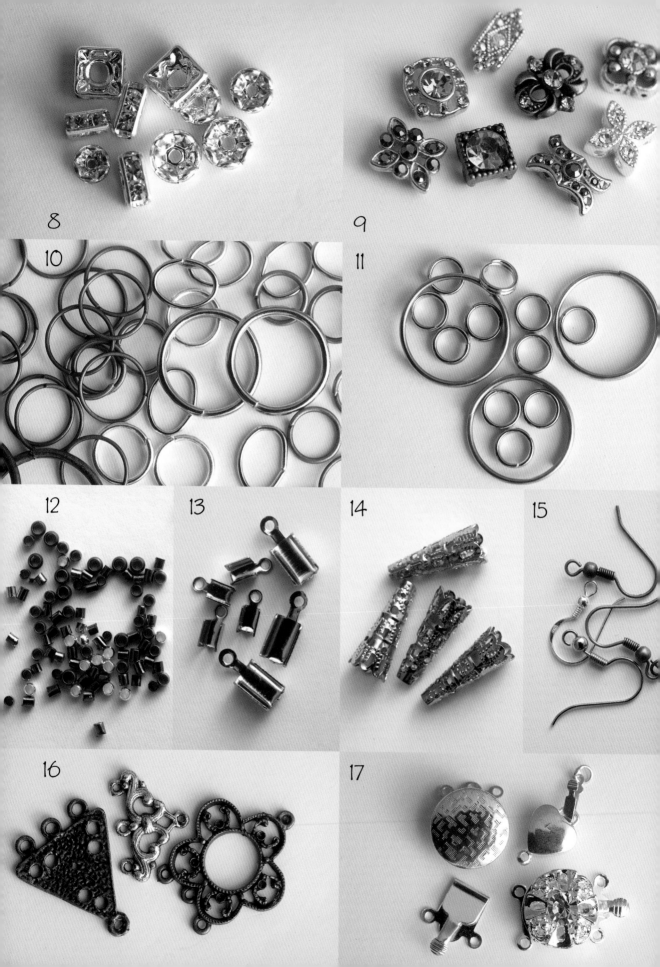

8

9

10

11

12

13

14

15

16

17

8 Swarovski spacers

Swarovski spacers are available in round and square shapes and contain Swarovski crystals. They are very exceptional and ideal for use with pearls or other Swarovski jewels.

9 Swarovski sliders

These sliders are available in many different styles and colors. They are usually highly decorative and can be used on their own or in combination with other beads.

10 Jump rings

Jump rings are used for connecting different parts of a piece of jewelry. The rings can be round or oval and are easy to bend open and closed. They, too, come in different sizes, thicknesses and colors. Choose the correct jump rings for the type of jewelry you are making, i.e., not too thick and large or too thin and small for your specific piece. Jump rings can also be used on their own for creating very interesting jewelry — an art form known as chain mail.

11 Split rings

Unlike jump rings, split rings cannot be bent open. They are similar in appearance to the rings found on key holders. To connect something to a split ring, it must be fed in the way a key would be fed onto a key ring. Split rings can be used at the ends of a piece of jewelry where fasteners are to be attached. Like all other findings, split rings come in different sizes, colors and thicknesses.

12 Crimp beads

Crimp beads are used for attaching beading thread to clasps or other fasteners. It is important to choose a size that is suitable for the thickness of the thread and the size of the beads. Always use good-quality crimp beads — it can be very frustrating when a crimp bead disintegrates after your beads have been strung with painstaking care.

13 Cord crimp ends

Cord crimp ends are used for finishing off the ends of cord or string. The cord ends are inserted into the crimp ends and then crimped tightly. A drop of glue can be used together with the crimp end to ensure that the cord or string remains secure.

14 Cones

Cones are most often used with multistrands, holding all the ends together and providing a particularly neat finish. Apart from being functional, they can also be very decorative. They come in different sizes and colors.

Earring components

There are numerous components on the market for making earrings, in a myriad of colors, sizes, patterns and shapes! By making interesting choices, extraordinary pieces can be created using a minimal number of beads.

15 Ear wires

Ear wires are available in various sizes and colors.

16 Other earring components

There are numerous components on the market for making earrings, in a myriad of colors, sizes, patterns and shapes! By making interesting choices, extraordinary pieces can be created using a minimal number of beads.

17 Clasps and fasteners

There are many different clasps and fasteners available, and your choice will be determined by the type of jewelry you are making. Once again it is very important to use good-quality fasteners, which will add value to your pieces and help ensure that they do not get lost.

The fastener should complement the specific piece of jewelry — large fasteners are suitable for bulky pieces, while a fine bracelet will be enhanced by a small fastener such as a toggle clasp.

18 Trigger clasp

This is the type of fastener that is most frequently used in jewelry making. Its spring action makes it easy to open and close, and it is generally also the cheapest on the market. An extension chain can be used in conjunction with these fasteners. They come in various colors and sizes, the larger ones being suitable for bag jewels and key holders.

19 Magnetic clasp

Magnetic clasps are handy to use, being extremely easy to open and close. They are not suitable for particularly heavy beads, however, as they can easily become undone and your jewelry may get lost.

20 Toggle clasp

This simple fastening mechanism is suitable for bracelets as well as necklaces. It comes in a large variety — choose the correct size for your specific piece.

21 Multistrand clasp

These clasps are used on multistrands in order to keep the strands separate.

22 Wrap clasp

These clasps fasten very securely and are particularly suitable for watches. Some wrap clasps also have a magnetic action, which together with the wrapping action makes them much safer than an ordinary magnetic clasp.

Tools

The only tools discussed here are the basic pliers you will need for beadwork. As with findings, a complete discussion of tools could very likely take up a whole book by itself. However, if you are a beading enthusiast, you will probably know that a few basic tools can go quite a long way.

23 Crimping pliers

Crimping pliers are used for neatly closing crimp beads. Ordinary flat-nose pliers can also be used for this, but crimping pliers give a more professional finish. The part closest to the handles neatly divides the bead into two, while the nose folds it over tightly.

24 Wire cutters

Invest in good-quality wire cutters right from the outset. Beadwork requires a lot of cutting, and inferior cutters will be blunt in no time. Buy fine-nose cutters suitable for delicate and accurate cutting. Wire that is not cut neatly can scratch and irritate the wearer of the jewelry.

25 Round-nose pliers

These are used for making eyelets, and are an indispensable piece of equipment.

26 Flat-nose (chain-nose) pliers

These are used for tightly holding and accurately bending wires and rings. Buy flat-nose pliers with a smooth, unribbed finish that will not leave unsightly marks on rings and wires.

27 Curved round-nose pliers

These pliers are very useful for working in hard-to-reach places where intricate linking is concerned. Although not essential, they are an extremely handy piece of equipment.

Stringing material

Different people prefer different stringing materials. Once again, use the one that works best for you! Some beaders do not like fishing line at all, while others won't come near tigertail. Just make sure that the material you choose is suitable for your project.

Cheap stringing material should never be used for real pearls — rather, choose a product that is specifically manufactured for the purpose. The sales staff in your local bead store will be able to offer the best advice.

Recommended stringing materials are indicated for each individual project in this book.

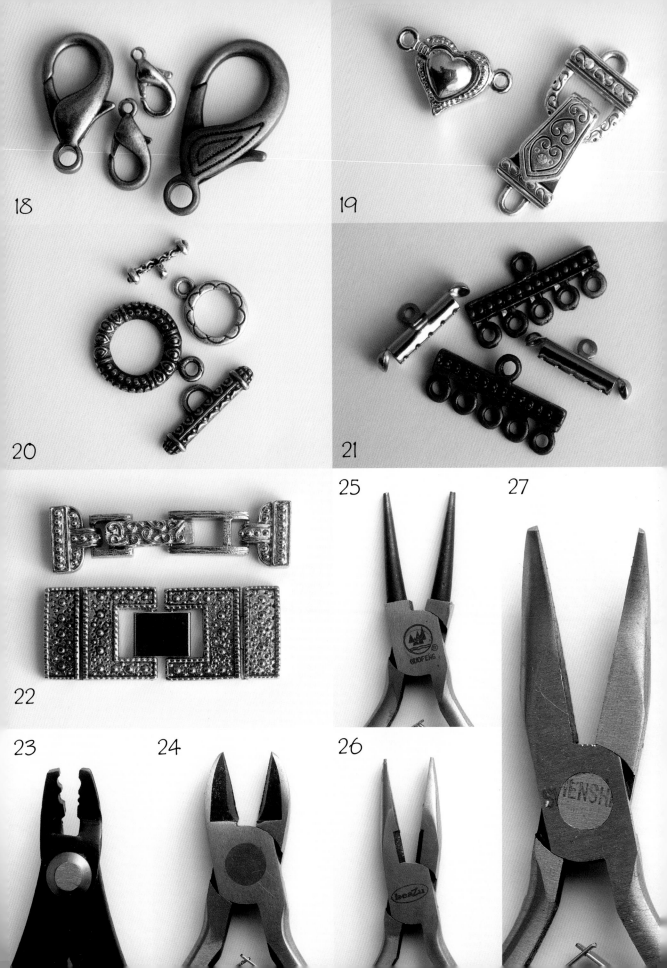

18

19

20

21

22

23

24

25

26

27

Types of beads

There is a vast variety of beads on the market, and it is expanding day by day. Every time I set foot in a bead store, I am amazed at the number of new beads and components I am exposed to. The beads used for the projects in this book are fairly readily available, but nothing prevents you from substituting them with unusual finds to create your own unique pieces. The types of beads discussed here are literally just the tip of the iceberg — only those you will come across in the book. There are zillions more to choose from.

1 Pearls

Pearls originate when a foreign object, such as a grain of sand, finds its way into an oyster shell. The object causes irritation to the soft inside of the oyster, which reacts by secreting a layer of calcium carbonate around the foreign object. Several layers of calcium carbonate are deposited, leading to the formation of a natural pearl. Natural pearls are extremely rare and expensive, as it takes up to eight years for an oyster to produce one pearl.

Cultured pearls are cheaper because they are produced in controlled conditions. A foreign object is deliberately placed inside the oyster, which is kept under close surveillance until a pearl is formed.

Freshwater pearls are cultured in freshwater mussels, which can produce up to 20 pearls per harvest. The pearls are harvested every one to two years. Rice pearls, available in a variety of shapes and colors, are the most common freshwater pearls.

2 Glass beads

Glass beads also come in various shapes and colors. An easy way to determine whether a bead is made from glass or plastic is to hold it against your upper lip. Glass beads will always feel cold, while plastic beads generally take on the temperature of the environment.

Pressed glass beads are made by casting molten glass into a mold to produce a specific shape. Machines are also used to press molten glass into desired shapes. Holes are then drilled through the width or length of the beads.

3 Seed beads

Seed beads, available in different shapes and colors, vary greatly in quality. The best seed beads, originating from Japan, are considerably more expensive than those from China and India. The Japanese beads are more evenly shaped, making them the perfect choice for loom beadwork. Seed-bead sizes are indicated by a number followed by a ° symbol. The larger the number, the smaller the bead. The sizes most commonly used are 8° and 11°.

4 Clay beads

Clay beads are available in various shapes and sizes. Roses and leaves are especially useful for creating some really special pieces.

5 Fire-polished beads

Fire-polished beads, varying in size from 3 mm to 22 mm, originate from the Czech Republic and are very popular in jewelry making. As the facets are identical for large and small beads, the latter often appear oval shaped. After being faceted by machines, the beads are fired in a red-hot furnace.

6 Swarovski crystals

These crystals are my undisputed favourite. Unfortunately they are fairly pricey, but they make the most exquisite jewelry! Swarovski crystals contain a minimum of 32 percent lead, allowing them to be precision-cut in a variety of shapes. The crystals, which have a fabulous luster, are multifaceted in order to reflect the maximum amount of light. As styles and colors become discontinued, their value increases.

Special finishes are sometimes used to further enhance the luster of Swarovski crystals, the most popular being Aurora Borealis, better known as AB. Other popular finishes are Vitrail and Heliotrope.

Although Swarovski crystals come in a large variety of shapes, colors and finishes, bicone crystals ranging from 3 mm to 10 mm in diameter are used most frequently.

Chinese crystals

Chinese crystals are flat, faceted crystals that are similar in appearance to spacers. Used in a number of projects in this book, they can be very effectively employed as spacers, but look just as attractive in a string of their own. They have a magnificent luster and are available in various colors.

7 Metal beads

As metal beads are becoming more and more popular, the variety is also expanding. Metal beads lend an interesting finish to jewelry, adding an exceptional touch to glass and other beads.

6

Mostly metal

There is a vast variety of metal beads on the market today, which, in conjunction with chains, can be used to create ravishing jewelry. If you have mastered the art of wirework, you can even make them yourself — visit bead stores for ideas to produce your own original ware.

Chains also come in an increasing variety of textures and unusual colors, such as blue, red and pink.

Charming crystal chain
The copper decorative chain has been combined with Swarovski crystals in various colors and can be worn with just about any outfit.

Silver heart chain
The collection of hearts on this silver chain makes for a striking piece.

Natural copper chain
Interesting metal beads combined with glass beads on a simple metal chain.

Glass pearls on silver chain

Easy to make, it is worn doubled up with the beaded ends passed through the chain loop.

Copper charms

A striking combination of assorted copper charms, pearls and small glass beads.

Chain with glass and metal charms

The charms you choose and the way in which the silver chain is used make this necklace unusual.

Charming crystal chain

When I came upon this unusual chain in a bead store, I just knew it would make for an extraordinary piece. Being so pretty in itself, very little glamming up is needed to create something special. Combined with round Swarovski crystals in a variety of hues, the chain will match most colors in your wardrobe.

Requirements:

- 1 m decorative chain
- 20 x 6 mm round Swarovski crystals in 5 different colors (pale blue, pink, silver shade, golden shadow, pale orange)
- 20 eyepins
- Round-nose pliers
- Flat-nose pliers
- Wire cutters

Method:

1. Thread each crystal onto an eyepin, then make a second eyelet on the opposite side of the crystal so that you have one eyelet on either side of each crystal.

2. Cut the chain halfway between two flowers.

3. Remove the two pieces of cut chain link.

4. Connect a crystal to each cut end.

5. Repeat, using a different color crystal each time, until all the crystals have been used.

Silver heart chain

The collection of hearts on this silver chain makes for a striking piece. This particular necklace was made by Settie.

Requirements:

- 1 m large-linked chain
- 2 trigger clasps
- 1 large silver heart
- Selection of silver heart charms
- Silver leaf charms
- Crystal heart charms
- Enough jump rings to connect charms to chain
- Round-nose pliers
- Flat-nose pliers

Method:

1. Connect a jump ring to each charm, leaving the rings open.
2. Connect the large silver heart to the middle of the chain, slipping the jump ring through the chain link, then closing the ring.

3. Securely connect the rest of the charms to the chain links, arranging them symmetrically on either side of the large heart.

4. Attach the crystal hearts in between.

5. Attach a trigger clasp to each end of the chain so that the chain length can be varied. The shorter you want the chain, the farther apart the clasps are hooked into the chain links.

Natural copper chain

A variety of interesting metal beads is combined with a simple metal chain to create this compliment-evoking neckpiece. Large glass beads in soft apricot and shiny brown glass pearls serve to soften the metallic look.

Requirements:

- 50 cm medium-linked copper chain
- Assorted metal beads (see photographs)
- 5 x 10 mm faceted glass beads (pale apricot)
- 5 x 4 mm glass pearls (brown)
- 10 bead caps to fit glass beads (copper)
- 60 eyepins (copper)
- Round-nose pliers
- Flat-nose pliers
- Wire cutters

Method:

1. Cut the chain into 10 lengths of 10 links each.

2. Thread each metal bead except wire beads onto an eyepin; make a second eyelet on opposite side of the bead so there is one eyelet on either side.

3. Using bead caps on either side, make eyelets for the glass beads as well.

4. Arrange the beads in groups, except the wire beads, then link them together before connecting them to the 10 cm lengths of chain.

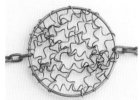

5. Attach 10 cm lengths of chain to either side of the wire beads and insert into the chain at regular intervals.

Glass pearls on silver chain

Substitute the silver chain and champagne pearls and beads of this quick and easy necklace with a brass or copper chain and beads and pearls in shades of olive green, brown or orange for an equally attractive piece. Wear it doubled up, with the two beaded ends taken through the loop, as shown in the picture.

Requirements:

- 1 m medium-linked silver chain
- 2 x 10 mm glass beads (champagne)
- 2 x 15 mm glass beads (champagne)
- 2 x 20 mm glass pearls (champagne)
- 4 eyepins (silver)
- 2 headpins (silver)
- 2 daisy spacers (silver)
- 6 Bali-silver spacers, 3 mm wide
- Round-nose pliers
- Flat-nose pliers
- Wire cutters

3. Thread a 15 mm bead, followed by a Bali-silver spacer, onto an eyepin, then make a second eyelet on the opposite side.

4. Connect the large glass pearl to the 15 mm bead by linking the eyelets.

Method:

1. Thread a daisy spacer, large glass pearl and Bali-silver spacer onto a headpin.

2. Make an eyelet above the spacer.

5. Thread a 10 mm bead, followed by a Bali-silver spacer, onto an eyepin, then make a second eyelet on the opposite side.

6. Link the small bead to the other beads, then connect all three to one end of the chain.

7. Repeat steps 1–6 for the remaining end of the chain.

Copper charms

The beautiful combination of assorted copper charms, pearls and small glass beads makes this necklace very special. Small side chains connected to the primary chain add to the effect. The string depicted here is very "full," the central large heart being flanked by numerous charms and chains. Small organza bows add extra interest.

Requirements:

No specific quantities are given, as this is merely an example you can use for creating a unique piece. Have fun!

- 50 cm medium-linked copper chain
- Assorted copper charms (see photographs)
- Some pearls and glass beads
- Eyepins in various lengths (copper)
- Headpins in various lengths (copper)
- Jump rings (copper)
- Trigger clasp (copper)
- Organza ribbon (brown)
- Round-nose pliers
- Flat-nose pliers
- Wire cutters

Method:

1. Start by preparing all the side chains and charms to be connected to the primary chain. Use headpins, eyepins and bits of chain.

2. Attach jump rings to all components to be connected to the chain.

3. Carefully plan the positioning of the components along the primary chain.

4. Attach the fastener to the ends of the chain.

5. First connect the larger charms to the chain, then fill up with the smaller components.

6. Tie three or four organza bows strategically along the chain.

Chain with glass and metal charms

This chain with glass and metal charms takes little effort and few materials to make, its uniqueness lying in the choice of the charms you use. The combination of unusual charms is extremely effective, with the clasp at the front of the necklace adding an interesting dimension. Use crystals for a special occasion.

Requirements:

- 60 cm large-linked silver chain
- 1 large trigger clasp
- 1 x 15 mm jump ring
- 6 x 8 mm jump rings
- 2 short headpins
- 1 bail
- 1 large glass drop
- 1 x 10 mm faceted glass bead
- 1 x 15 mm silver ball
- 1 x 25 mm drop
- 1 x 40 mm drop
- 90 cm fine silver chain
- Flat-nose pliers

Method:

1. Cut the fine chain into 10 lengths of approximately 9 cm each, then insert all 10 into a small jump ring.
2. Connect the bail to the large drop, then insert into a small jump ring.
3. Thread the silver ball and faceted glass bead onto separate headpins, then make an eyelet for each (see page 8).
4. Connect a small jump ring to the silver ball and the faceted glass beads.
5. Using a small jump ring, attach the trigger clasp to one end of the chain. Attach the large jump ring to the other end.
6. Insert the fine chains, silver ball, large drop and remaining beads into the large jump ring, then close the ring securely.
7. The fastener can be hooked either into the large jump ring or, alternatively, higher up along the chain, allowing the charms to dangle on a single length of chain (see diagram).

Bracelets

Worn by the Romans and Egyptians since the earliest of times, bracelets were considered symbols of wealth and status. Kings and governors wore bracelets as a denotation of the position they held. These were often lavishly embellished with coins and other metal objects.

Today bracelets are worn mainly decoratively, and sometimes for medicinal reasons. Create your own to suit your personal taste and preference. If you are not quite ready to tackle a necklace yet, a bracelet is the perfect starting point.

Swarovski bracelets

These bracelets can be made in different color combinations and you can also vary the spacers.

Swarovski bracelets with flower sliders

All the samples have been made with two colors only, but a multi-colored bracelet is just as effective.

Smartie bracelet

Teens love this brightly colored bracelet that is threaded in no time onto beading elastic.

Multistrand crystal bracelet

Worn with the matching earrings on page 103, this is the ideal accessory for prom night.

Crystal and wire bracelet

Simply make the string longer and wider for a gorgeous necklace.

Delicate metal and crystal bracelet

An exceptional rose clasp enhances this simple combination and makes it really special.

Gray pearls and crystals on memory wire

A lovely combination of fairly light beads that will not overstretch the wire.

Pink and brown twisted strings

Three completely different strings make a good combination.

Sparkling crystal

This bracelet matches the crystal necklace on page 80. Good-quality glass beads will look just as attractive.

Blue cluster bracelet

A variety of beads, bead caps, metal charms and even buttons connected to a chain with additional embellishments in between.

Swarovski bracelets

The same method is followed for all the Swarovski bracelets photographed here, using different colors of crystals. In the instructions, colors are referred to as 1, 2 and 3, giving you the opportunity to assemble your own combinations. Use three identical sliders, or choose a different one for the center.

Requirements:

- 16 x 6 mm bicone crystals (color 1)
- 8 x 6 mm bicone crystals (color 2)
- 8 x 6 mm bicone crystals (color 3)
- 3 Swarovski sliders (silver)
- 28 spacers, at least 3 mm wide
- 1 toggle clasp
- 2 crimp beads
- Stringing material
  (tigertail or nylon yarn)
- 2 jump rings

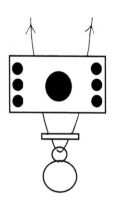

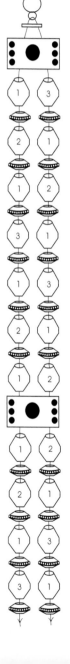

Method:

1. Thread the stringing material through one jump ring, doubling up the string.
2. Thread one crimp bread onto both strings simultaneously and firmly pinch the crimp bead closed.
3. Thread one slider onto both strings simultaneously.
4. Now thread the crystals onto the two separate strings as follows: **First string:** color 1, spacer, color 2, spacer, color 1, spacer, color 3, spacer, color 1, spacer, color 2, spacer, color 1, spacer, color 3; **Second string:** color 2, spacer, color 1, spacer, color 3, spacer, color 1, spacer, color 2, spacer, color 1, spacer, color 3, spacer, color 1.
5. Thread the central slider onto both strings simultaneously.
6. Continue threading the first string as follows: color 3, spacer, color 1, spacer, color 2, spacer, color 1, spacer, color 3, spacer, color 1, spacer, color 2, spacer, color 1. (Forming a mirror image on either side of the central slider, this string begins and ends with color 1.)
7. Continue threading the second string as follows: color 1, spacer, color 3, spacer, color 1, spacer, color 2, spacer, color 1, spacer, color 3, spacer, color 1, spacer, color 2. (Forming a mirror image on either side of the central slider, this string begins and ends with color 2.)
8. Thread the final slider onto both strings simultaneously.
9. Thread the remaining crimp bead onto both strings simultaneously, then thread the strings through the remaining jump ring and back through the crimp bread again.
10. Firmly pinch the crimp bead closed.
11. Attach the two halves of the toggle clasp to either end of the bracelet.

Swarovski bracelet with flower sliders

Elastic can also be used as stringing material, but the weight of the sliders may cause it to lose its elasticity too quickly. Choose your own colors — although instructions are given for two colors only, a multicolored bracelet can look very attractive.

Requirements:

- 8 flower sliders
- 14 x 6 mm bicone Swarovski crystals (color 1)
- 14 x 6 mm bicone Swarovski crystals (color 2)
- 1 toggle clasp
- 50 cm stringing material (tigertail or nylon yarn)
- 2 crimp beads
- 2 jump rings

Method:

1. Thread the stringing material through one jump ring, doubling up the string. Thread both strings through a crimp bead and close the bead firmly.

2. Thread a color 1 crystal followed by color 2 onto one string, then thread a color 2 crystal followed by color 1 onto the other.

3. Thread both strings through one slider.

4. Now thread the crystals onto the two separate strings as in step 2, followed by a spacer (both strings through one). Alternate the sequence if you wish.

5. Repeat five more times, ending with crystals.

6. Thread both strings through the remaining crimp bread, then thread the strings through the remaining jump ring and back through the crimp bread. Close the crimp bead.

7. Attach the two sections of the toggle clasp to either end of the bracelet.

Smartie bracelet

My teenage daughters immediately fell in love with this brightly colored bracelet, bullying me into making another so that they could each have their own. It takes two seconds to complete, and because it is strung on elastic, no meticulous measuring is required.

Requirements:

- 12 round mother-of-pearl smartie beads (various colors)
- 12 square mother-of-pearl smartie beads (various colors)
- 6 multistrand spacers with 5 or 7 holes
- 50 cm firm elastic
- Quick-drying glue

Method:

1. Cut the elastic in two, then loosely knot the strings together at one end.

2. Thread the elastic strings through a spacer individually, threading each string through the second hole from the edge.

3. Thread a round bead onto string 1 and a square bead onto string 2.

4. Thread a square bead onto string 1 and a round bead onto string 2.

5. Thread both elastic strings through another spacer.

6. Repeat steps 3 and 4 five more times, undo the knot in the elastics, then tie each string separately (see page 9).

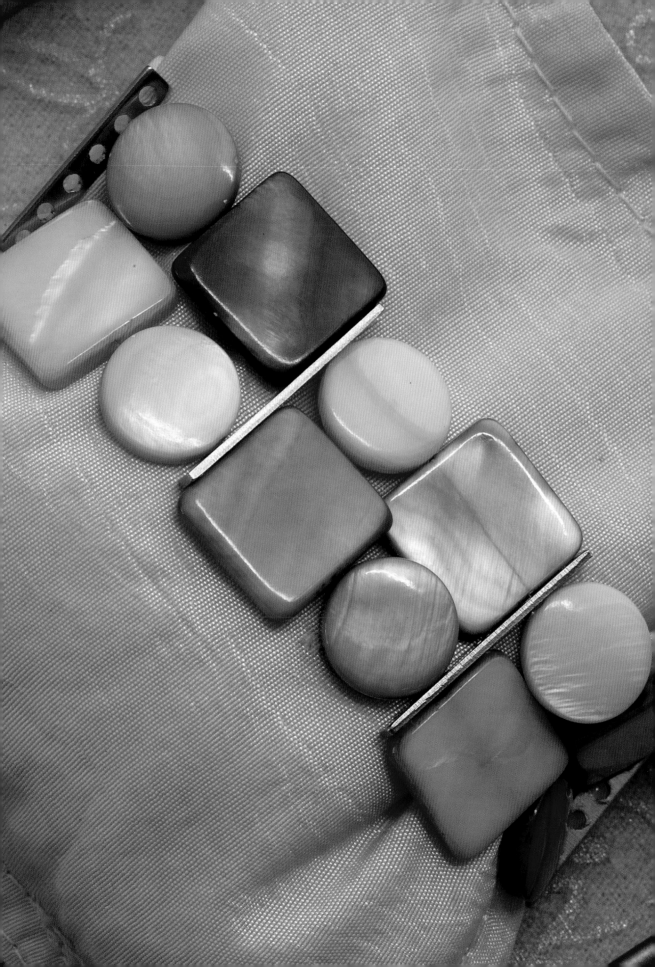

Multistrand crystal bracelet

Worn with the matching earrings on page 103, this quick and easy bracelet is the ideal accessory for prom night or a graduation dance. To create a unique piece of jewelry, follow the basic instructions using beads and colors of your own choice.

Requirements:

- 50 Chinese crystals (olive green)
- 22 x 4 mm bicone Swarovski crystals (khaki)
- 33 x 4 mm bicone Swarovski crystals (golden shadow)
- 33 x 4 mm bicone Swarovski crystals (olivine)
- 15 x 6 mm bicone Swarovski crystals (golden shadow)
- 15 x 6 mm bicone Swarovski crystals (pale topaz)
- 1 m stringing elastic
- 20 cm narrow organza ribbon (champagne)

Method:

1. Cut the elastic into four lengths of 25 cm each.

2. **String 1:** thread all the Chinese crystals onto one length of elastic and finish off with a knot (see page 9).

3. **String 2:** thread 3 x 4 mm golden shadow, then 1 x 4 mm khaki crystals. Repeat 10 more times and finish off as for the previous string.

4. **String 3:** thread 3 x 4 mm olivine, then 1 x 4 mm khaki crystals. Repeat 10 more times and finish off as for the previous strings.

5. **String 4:** thread 1 x 6 mm golden shadow, then 1 x 6 mm pale topaz crystals. Repeat 14 more times and finish off as for the previous strings.

6. Tie all four strings with the organza ribbon, make a bow and trim the ribbon ends diagonally.

Crystal and wire bracelet

This bracelet is made up of 6 mm Swarovski crystals and jump rings. For a gorgeous necklace, simply make the string longer and wider. The Swarovski crystals can be substituted with faceted glass beads to create an equally pretty piece.

Requirements:

- 41 x 6 mm bicone Swarovski crystals (blue zircon)
- 1 trigger clasp with extension chain (copper)
- 40 eyepins (copper)
- 1 headpin
- 21 jump rings (copper)
- Round-nose pliers
- Flat-nose pliers

Method:

1. Thread each crystal onto an eyepin; make a second eyelet on the opposite side of the crystal so that you have one eyelet on either side of each crystal.

2. Open a jump ring, insert four crystals, then close the ring again.

3. Opening another jump ring, insert one crystal from the first ring plus three new crystals. Close the ring. Repeat until you have 10 groups of crystals.

4. Opening yet another jump ring, insert crystals as follows: one new, two from the previous groups, one new. Repeat 9 more times.

5. Connect a jump ring to either end of the bracelet. Attach the fastener, then finish off the extension chain with a 6 mm crystal, using a headpin.

Gray pearls and crystals on memory wire

Memory wire is a fairly thick coil wire available in bracelet and necklace lengths. The extensible wire always returns to its original length, hence the name "memory wire." The pearls and crystals form a pretty combination, with crystal ends lending a finishing touch. These can be replaced by silver balls glued to the ends of the wire. Choose beads with care, as heavy beads may cause overstretching of the wire.

Requirements:

- 20 x 8 mm glass pearls (pale gray)
- 10 x 8 mm glass pearls (medium gray)
- 18 x 2 mm silver beads
- 9 x 6 mm round Swarovski crystals (black diamond)
- 4 x 8 mm bicone Swarovski crystals (black diamond)
- 4 x 4 mm bicone Swarovski crystals (black diamond)
- 4 round Swarovski spacers
- 4 headpins
- Round-nose pliers
- Flat-nose pliers
- Wire cutters

Method:

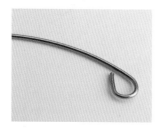

1. Make an eyelet in one end of the memory wire.

2. Thread the pearls, crystals and silver beads onto the wire as follows: pale gray pearl, medium gray pearl, pale gray pearl, silver bead, round crystal, silver bead.

3. Repeat eight more times, ending with a pale gray pearl.

4. Make an eyelet in the other end of the wire, then trim the excess wire using wire cutters.

5. Thread an 8 mm crystal, followed by a spacer and a 4 mm crystal, onto a headpin, then make an eyelet.

6. Make four of these combinations, then connect two to either end of the bracelet.

Sparkling crystal

This bracelet is made to match the crystal necklace on page 80. Swarovski crystals are fairly expensive, but good-quality glass beads will look equally attractive. Achromatic jewelry is highly versatile and can be worn with almost any color.

Requirements:

- 126 x 4 mm bicone Swarovski crystals (crystal AB)
- 2 x 6 mm bicone Swarovski crystals (crystal AB)
- 5 Swarovski multistrand spacers with 3 holes
- 4 plain multistrand spacers with 3 holes
- 4 crimp beads (sterling silver)
- Toggle clasp (sterling silver)
- 2 jump rings (sterling silver)
- 2 shell ends (sterling silver)
- 90 cm stringing material (tigertail or nylon yarn)
- Crimping pliers

Steps 2–5

Method:

1. Cut the stringing material into 3 x 30 cm lengths.
2. Thread strings through a crimp bead, a shell end and back through the crimp bead.
3. Thread all three strings through a 6 mm Swarovski crystal, followed by a second crimp bead.
4. Firmly close the crimp bead as explained on page 9.
5. Thread each string through a plain multistand spacer, one string though each hole.
6. **First string:** 4 x 4 mm crystals.
   Second string: 3 x 4 mm crystals.
   Third string: 2 x 4 mm crystals.
7. Thread each string through a plain multistrand spacer.
8. **First string:** 4 x 4 mm crystals.
   Second string: 6 x 4 mm crystals.
   Third string: 8 x 4 mm crystals.
9. Thread each string through a Swarovski multistrand spacer.
10. **First string:** 8 x 4 mm crystals.
    Second string: 6 x 4 mm crystals.
    Third string: 4 x 4 mm crystals.
11. Thread each string through a Swarovski multistrand spacer.
12. Repeat steps 8–11, then steps 8–10 once more.
13. Thread each string through a plain multistrand spacer.
14. **First string:** 2 x 4 mm crystals.
    Second string: 3 x 4 mm crystals.
    Third string: 4 x 4 mm crystals.
15. Thread each string through a plain multistrand spacer.
16. Thread all three strings through a crimp bead, then firmly close the crimp bead.
17. Thread all three strings through a 6 mm Swarovski crystal.
18. Finish off as for the beginning.
19. Connect a jump ring to the shell end on either end of the bracelet, then attach the two halves of the toggle clasp.

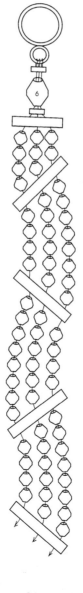

Delicate metal and crystal bracelet

This delicate bracelet is beautifully complemented by its exceptional rose clasp. The metal bars are also available in antique silver and silver base metal.

Requirements:

- 20 curved metal bars (copper)
- 9 x 6 mm round Swarovski crystals (topaz)
- 40 x 4 mm bicone Swarovski crystals (peridot)
- 45 x 11° seed beads (peach)
- Rose clasp (copper)
- 50 cm nylon yarn
- Crimping pliers

Method:

1. Cut the nylon yarn in two, then loosely knot the strings together at one end. Be sure to leave ample slack.

2. Thread the first string as follows: seed bead, metal bar end, seed bead, bicone crystal x 2, seed bead, metal bar end, seed bead, round crystal.

3. Repeat for the second string, threading the second string through the same round crystal as for the first string, but from the opposite side.

4. Repeat until all the round crystals have been used.

5. Continue by threading each string as follows: seed bead, metal bar end, seed bead, bicone crystal x 2, seed bead, metal bar end, seed bead.

6. Thread a seed bead, followed by a crimp bead, onto both strings simultaneously.

7. Thread the strings through one half of the clasp, then back through the crimp bead. Firmly pinch the crimp bead closed, then thread the strings back through at least five beads.

8. Undo the knot, then repeat steps 5–7 on the remaining end of the bracelet.

Pink and brown twisted strings

The three strings form a pretty combination, one being completely different from the rest. Wear them twisted together, or keep the strings separated. The pink and brown lend a soft and feminine air.

Requirements:

- 2 large multifaceted resin beads (pink)
- 2 large matte glass beads (pink)
- 4 bead caps to fit large glass beads (copper)
- 5 x 6 mm fisheye beads (pink)
- 6 x 4 mm fisheye beads (pink)
- 5 x 8 mm clear glass beads (pink)
- 25 x 3 mm pearls (pink)
- 5 x 4 mm pearls (brown)
- 20 x 2 mm beads (brown)
- 4 oval glass beads (pink)
- 12 small bead caps (copper)
- 2 jump rings (copper)
- 1 toggle clasp (copper)
- 60 cm tigertail (brown)
- 6 crimp beads (copper)
- Crimping pliers
- Flat-nose pliers

Method:

1. Cut the tigertail into three lengths of 20 cm each.
2. Thread one crimp bead onto each string, then thread the three strings through one jump ring and then back through the individual crimp beads again.
3. Firmly pinch the crimp beads closed.
4. Now thread the three strings as follows:

   First string: 8 mm pink glass bead, 4 mm pink fisheye, pink resin bead, 4 mm pink fisheye, 8 mm pink glass bead, bead cap, matte pink glass bead, bead cap. Repeat once more, ending with an 8 mm glass bead.

   Second string: 2 mm brown bead, 6 mm pink fisheye, 2 mm brown bead, 3 mm pink pearl, bead cap, pink oval, bead cap, 3 mm pink pearl. Repeat three more times, ending with a 6 mm pink fisheye followed by a 2 mm brown bead.

   Third string: 3 mm pink pearl, 2 mm brown bead, 3 mm pink pearl, 2 mm brown bead, 3 mm pink pearl, 4 mm brown pearl, 3 mm pink pearl, 2 mm brown bead, 3 mm pink pearl, 4 mm brown pearl, 3 mm pink pearl, 2 mm brown bead, 3 mm pink pearl, 2 mm brown bead, bead cap, 4 mm pink fisheye, bead cap, 3 mm pink pearl, 4 mm brown pearl. This is the center of the string. To complete, change the sequence to a mirror image of the first half.
5. Finish off as for the beginning, then attach the two halves of the toggle clasp to either end of the bracelet.

Blue cluster bracelet

Although the basic principles remain the same, cluster bracelets can be great fun to make. Using a variety of beads, bead caps, metal charms and even buttons, any number of strings and embellishments can be connected to the chain. The more different components you use, the more interesting the result will be.

The best thing about making a cluster bracelet is that you decide how "full" it must be. Fewer, smaller beads produce more conservative pieces, while larger quantities and components make for bulkier bracelets.

The following principles should be kept in mind when making a cluster bracelet:

1. Always begin by evenly spacing the largest beads along your chain.
2. Continue by evenly connecting the next size of beads, then the next, etc.
3. Finish off by filling the bracelet with smaller beads.

Use the photographs as inspiration for creating your own unique cluster bracelet. Have fun!

Magnet magic

Hematite beads can be magnetized, a particularly useful attribute when it comes to jewelry making. Apart from eliminating the use of fasteners, magnetic beads can be worn in different ways, depending on how they are arranged. Some people also believe that wearing magnetic jewelry holds health benefits.

Magnets and moonstone
This string is very simple to make and can be worn as a bracelet, necklace or choker.

With pearls and crystal
A combination of pearls, crystals and magnets forming a zigzag pattern makes this an unusual piece.

Magnets and moonstone

Comprising only one long strand, this moonstone string is very simple to make. It can be worn as either a bracelet or a necklace.

Requirements:

- 38 magnetic beads
- 78 x 4 mm round faceted moonstone beads
- 39 x 2 mm round faceted moonstone beads
- 80 flower spacers
- Nymo yarn, size D
- Beading needle

Method:

1. Thread the needle with the nymo yarn, leaving the yarn on the reel. This means you do not waste any thread, the thread does not get knotted and you don't need a stop bead.

2. Thread the string through a spacer and the following: 4 mm bead, spacer, 2 mm bead, spacer, 4 mm bead, magnetic bead.

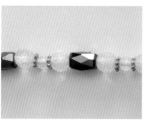

3. Repeat the sequence 37 more times, ending with a 4 mm bead, followed by a spacer, 2 mm bead, spacer, 4 mm bead and another spacer.

4. Taking the string over the last spacer, thread it back through all the beads until you reach the starting point. (The double string reinforces your piece.)

5. Cut the string, then knot the two ends together. Taking the string over the first spacer, thread it back through at least 10 beads.

Magnets with pearls and crystals

This bracelet is extremely easy to make, requiring just simple threading. What makes it so special is the combination of crystals, pearls and magnetic beads. The zigzag pattern is the result of the pearls being larger than the magnetic beads. Although this is essentially a bracelet, it can also be worn as a necklace — wrap the string around your neck twice, or hang it around your neck as for a scarf, pressing the magnets on the two loose ends together.

Requirements:

- 20 x 8 mm pearls (olive green)
- 21 magnetic beads
- 80 x 4 mm Swarovski crystals (40 khaki, 40 vitrail)
- 160 flower spacers (silver)
- 40 small filigree beads (silver)
- 2 x 11° seed beads (green)
- Nymo yarn, size D
- Beading needle

Method:

1. Thread the needle with the nymo yarn, leaving the yarn on the reel. (The yarn is unwound as the beads are threaded, saving you yarn and preventing the string from getting entangled.)

2. Thread the string through a seed bead and the following: magnetic bead, spacer, khaki crystal, spacer, vitrail crystal, spacer, filigree bead, spacer, pearl, spacer, filigree bead, spacer, vitrail crystal, spacer, khaki crystal, spacer.

3. Repeat 19 more times, ending with a magnetic bead.

4. Thread the string through a seed bead, over and back through all the beads until you reach the starting point. (The double string reinforces it.)

5. Cut the string, then knot the two ends together. Taking the string over the first seed bead, thread it back through at least 10 beads.

Quick 'n easy

These instant pieces will take you no longer than half an hour or an hour to make. With the beads and Swarovski sliders as pretty as they are, it is a good idea to simply thread them onto elastic or other stringing material.

Keep in mind that quick and easy does not always mean cheap. Truly exceptional beads can be quite expensive, but you can bank on an elegant and stylish result.

Quick slider bracelets

These bracelets are about 16–18 cm long. Measure your wrist before you begin to determine how many sliders you will need.

Bracelet with hematites and crystal

The color of hematite matches most other bead colors exceptionally well, making it the perfect coordinate for a variety of beads.

Light and casual

An interesting combination of textile, Bali-silver and fisheye beads makes for this striking, peppy piece.

Blue and white strands

The bead strands are threaded separately, but make a really striking impression when worn together.

Simple lariats

Really easy to make, this is the perfect project for the beginner.

Multistrand rope

Nine to 10 individual strings comprising only seed and tiny bugle beads, strung randomly so no two strings look exactly the same.

Quick slider bracelets

These bracelets are approximately 16–18 cm long. Measure your wrist before you begin to determine how many sliders you will need.

Requirements:

- Approximately 2 x 35 cm elastic (this is much more than you will actually need, but easier to handle)
- Sliders to fit around your wrist
- Quick-drying glue

Method:

1. Thread the sliders onto the elastic and finish off with a knot (see page 9).
2. If the sliders you are using are fairly heavy, thread the elastic through the beads twice, or use a double length of elastic from the outset.

Bracelet with hematites and crystals

Hematite beads lend a lavish appearance to any jewelry and are wonderfully cool to the touch. Their color matches most colors exceptionally well, making them the perfect coordinate for a variety of other beads. The blue crystals used here look fresh and cool.

Requirements:

- 70 cm firm elastic
- 32 x 6 mm bicone Swarovski crystals (pale blue)
- 8 round hematite spacers with 2 holes
- 16 small hematite cubes
- Quick-drying glue

Method:

1. Cut two lengths of elastic, approximately 35 cm each, and loosely knot them together at one end.
2. Thread a spacer onto both elastics.
3. Now thread each string as follows: blue crystal, hematite cube, blue crystal.
4. Thread the next spacer onto both elastics.
5. Repeat steps 3 and 4 six more times, then end off with step 3.
6. Undo the knot in the elastics, then knot each elastic separately (see page 9).

Light and casual

An interesting combination of textile, Bali-silver and fisheye beads makes for this striking, peppy piece. No fasteners are required, as the string is long enough to simply pull over your head. The recommended cord has a wax coating, making it particularly strong and easy to work with, as it hardly frays. The pendant can either be left out — the necklace will look pretty enough on its own — or replaced with an adornment of your choice.

Requirements:

- 50 cm waxed cord (white)
- 32 x 6 mm Bali-silver beads
- 8 tubular fisheye beads (white)
- 8 x 6 mm round fisheye beads (white)
- 7 large round seeded beads (purple pink)
- 8 textile beads (green and silver)
- 1 decorative pendant
- Quick-drying glue

Method:

1. Starting with a large round bead, thread the rest of the beads as follows: Bali-silver, round fisheye, Bali-silver, green textile, Bali-silver, tubular fisheye, Bali-silver.
2. Repeat the sequence three more times, then add the pendant.
3. Now change the sequence to a mirror image of the first half: Bali-silver, tubular fisheye, Bali-silver, green textile, Bali-silver, round fisheye, Bali-silver, large round.
4. Knot the cord and apply a drop of glue to the knot. Trim away the excess cord, then pull the knot into the hole of the large round bead.

Blue and white strands

The bead strands are threaded separately, but make a striking impression when worn together. Both strands are extra long so that they can be worn in different ways. A single strand can be worn either hanging loose or wrapped around the neck twice.

Requirements:

- 2 m stringing material (nymo yarn) per string
- Blue and white beads in a variety of shapes and sizes
- Flower sequins for the white string
- Quick-drying glue

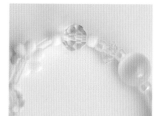

Method:

1. Arrange the beads for each string to form a pattern. Once you are happy with the sequence, thread the beads onto the stringing material until the required length is reached.
2. Finish off with a knot (see page 9). Add a drop of glue to the knot and pull back into one of the beads.

Simple lariats

If you are a beading enthusiast, you will probably be familiar with the lariat. Really easy to make, this is the perfect project for the beginner. With the right choice of beads, very attractive pieces can be created. Roses, metal beads, chains, buttons and interesting gemstone chips can also be used to add to the uniqueness of the piece.

These photographs show black and claret, brown and white lariats. Simple beading cord was used throughout, but decorative cord can be applied very effectively.

Requirements:

- 1.5 m beading cord or any other interesting cord
- Variety of beads

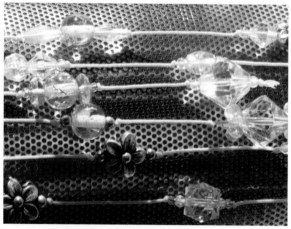

Method:

1. Apply clear nail polish or glue to approximately 1 cm of one cord end. Allow to dry completely, then cut the end diagonally to prevent the cord from fraying while the beads are being threaded.
2. Tie a standard knot in the other end.
3. Plan the combinations in which the beads are to be strung.

4. Thread the first combination onto the cord, then tie a knot right up against the beads.
5. Tie another knot approximately 5 cm away and thread the next combination of beads onto the cord.
6. Repeat until the required length is reached, then tie a knot right up against the last bead. Trim any excess cord close to the knot.

Multistrand rope with seed beads

This rope is made up of nine or 10 individual strings comprising only seed and tiny bugle beads, strung randomly so that no two strings look exactly the same. Glass bicones are used near the ends. For a multicolored rope, combine different colors of seed beads for each individual string, or use various monochromatic strings together. Seed beads and bugles of the same color can also be alternated.

Requirements:

- 100 g x 11° seed beads (pale green)
- 100 g x 3 mm bugle beads (pale green)
- 60 x 4 mm bicone glass beads (pale green)
- 10 m nymo yarn, size D
- Beading needle or bead spinner

(A bead spinner is ideal for threading long strings of seed beads. A bowl filled with beads is spun around, while a curved needle randomly picks up the beads.)

Method:

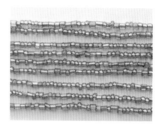

1. Thread seed and bugle beads onto nymo yarn, make nine to 10 strings of about 1 m each, alternating the order and combination of beads for each string.

2. Use 3 bicone glass beads near both ends of each string; alternate the space between the bicones. Use about 30 seed beads between bicones.

3. To finish the ends, thread the yarn through one more seed bead. Taking the yarn over the last seed bead, thread it back through approximately 5 cm of the bead string. Tie the end to the primary string, then pull the knot into the hole of an adjacent bead.

This versatile piece can be worn in different ways:

- Drape all the strings around your neck simultaneously and loosely knot them together.
- Wear the strings as a belt around your waist.
- Wrap the strings around your neck twice, letting the ends hang loose as for a scarf.

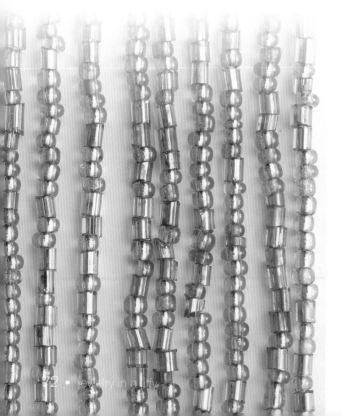

Pearls and crystals

Each with a charm of their own, pearls and crystals make for exceptional jewelry when used in combination. Pearls are usually strung on silk cord, available in different thicknesses. For ease of stringing, most silk cords come with a pre-threaded needle.

Classic cream
This necklace was made for my daughter to wear on her wedding day. Her jewelry was kept as plain as possible, the very beauty of the piece lying in its simplicity.

Black is beautiful
Black and other dark-colored pearls are divine and make exquisite jewelry combined with glass and crystal.

Lustrous crystal
Swarovski crystals are exquisite and elegant. For a piece of this nature a top-quality clasp is required.

Classic cream

This necklace was specially made for my daughter to wear on her wedding day. As her gown was adorned with an ornate lace bodice and sleeves, her jewelry had to be kept as plain as possible, the very beauty of the piece lying in its simplicity. It looked absolutely stunning on her! The Swarovski crystals have a splendid luster when light is reflected by their multiple facets. Instructions for the matching earrings can be found on page 98.

Requirements:

- 1 m silk cord with needle
- 28 x 6 mm bicone Swarovski crystals (golden shadow)
- 28 x 6-8 mm freshwater pearls (champagne)
- 56 flower spacers (antique silver)
- 2 shell ends (sterling silver)
- 1 clasp (sterling silver)
- 2 crimp beads (sterling silver)
- 2 small jump rings (sterling silver)
- Crimping pliers

Method:

1. Thread a stop bead onto the cord to prevent the beads from slipping off.
2. Thread the pearls, crystals and spacers as follows, until the required length is reached: spacer, crystal, spacer, pearl, spacer, crystal, etc.
3. Thread the cord through a shell end and crimp bead.
4. Threading the cord back through the shell end, pull the cord tight, allowing the crimp bead to settle in the hollow of the shell end.
5. Close the crimp bead and shell end.
6. Now thread the cord back through all the spacers, crystals and pearls until you reach the starting point. The double cord serves as reinforcement to prevent the beads from falling off in the event that one cord wears or breaks.
7. Remove the stop bead and finish off as for the other end, using a crimp bead and shell end.
8. Connect a jump ring to both ends, then complete the necklace by attaching the clasp.

Black is beautiful

Black and other dark-colored pearls are divine and make exquisite jewelry. For this piece, very dark pearls are combined with crystals to create an unusual effect. The string is longer than a normal string of pearls, but can be made shorter by simply using fewer pearls and crystals.

Requirements:

- 1 m silk cord with needle
- 48 x 8 mm dark pearls
- 45 x 8 mm faceted glass beads
- 60 flower spacers
- 30 Chinese crystals
- Beading needle (thin enough to pass through the pearls)
- 1 trigger clasp with extension chain
- 2 crimp beads (sterling silver)
- 2 shell ends (sterling silver)
- 1 jump ring
- Crimping pliers

Method:

1. Thread a stop bead onto the cord to prevent the beads from slipping off.
2. Thread the pearls, crystals and spacers as follows, until the required length is reached: pearls x 3, spacer, Chinese crystal, spacer, glass bead, spacer, Chinese crystal, spacer, etc.
3. Thread the cord through a shell end and crimp bead.

4. Threading the cord back through the shell end, pull the cord tight, allowing the crimp bead to settle in the hollow of the shell end.
5. Close the crimp bead and shell end.
6. Now thread the cord back through all the spacers, crystals and pearls until you reach the starting point. The double cord serves as reinforcement to prevent the beads from falling off in the event that one cord wears or breaks.
7. Remove the stop bead and finish off as for the other end, using a crimp bead and shell end.
8. Connect a jump ring to both ends, then complete the necklace by attaching the fastener.

Lustrous crystal

This beautiful necklace, made exclusively from Swarovski crystals, is exquisitely smart and elegant. Fit for a queen, it takes only half an hour to make! Because the crystals are fairly expensive, care must be taken to choose the best-quality clasp and bail, preferably sterling silver. The bracelet on page 50 makes the perfect coordinate for this piece.

Requirements:

- 1 large Swarovski crystal pendant (crystal)
- 90 x 3 mm bicone crystals (crystal)
- 10 x 4 mm bicone crystals (crystal AB)
- 20 x 4 mm round crystals (crystal AB)
- 1 toggle clasp adorned with crystals (sterling silver)
- 1 bail (sterling silver)
- 50 cm tigertail
- 2 crimp beads (sterling silver)
- Crimping pliers
- Wire cutters

Method:

1. Attach the tigertail to one half of the toggle clasp as follows: thread the tigertail through a crimp bead, then through the clasp opening and back through the crimp bead again.
2. Firmly pinch the crimp bead closed.
3. Connect the bail to the Swarovski pendant.
4. Thread the string as follows: 45 x 3 mm bicone crystals, 5 x 4 mm bicone crystals, 10 x 4 mm round crystals, pendant.
5. After the pendant, change the sequence to a mirror image of the first half: 10 x 4 mm round crystals, 5 x 4 mm bicone crystals, 45 x 3 mm bicone crystals.
6. Attach the remaining half of the toggle clasp to the end of the string as for the first half, using a crimp bead.

Versatile felt

I still vividly recall the felt art projects I made as a young girl. These included finger puppets and "paintings" made from felt shapes. Felt is a firm material, and easy to work with as it does not fray. Available in a variety of bright colors, it is often sold in squares of approximately 20 cm, eliminating the need for buying more than you will use.

Some bead stores sell ready-to-string felt beads, suitable to be used on their own or in combination with other beads.

Funky felt necklace

The brightly colored felt spirals and chunky beads are reminiscent of a string of candy! For a less bulky piece, apply the same technique using thinner fabric. Just make sure that your fabric does not fray.

Requirements:

- Felt squares (20 x 20 cm) in black and bright colors
- 7 large black glass beads with brightly colored detail
- 1.5 m black linen cord
- 26 x 6 mm onyx beads
- Black sewing thread
- Dressmaker's shears
- Dressmaker's pins
- Sharp-pointed needle

Method:

Start by making the felt beads as follows:

1. Cut six black felt strips of 2 x 12 cm each.

2. Cut six brightly colored felt strips of the same size.

3. Place a black and a colored strip on top of each other and roll up tightly.

4. Trim away the excess felt at the outside end.

5. Using black sewing thread, sew the end in place to maintain the spiral shape.

6. Thread the black linen cord through a sharp-pointed needle with a fairly large eye. Doubling up the cord, knot the loose ends together.

7. Thread groups of beads onto the string as follows: onyx bead, felt bead, onyx bead. Tie a knot right up against the onyx bead, followed by another knot 4 cm away, onyx bead, large glass bead, onyx bead. Add knots.

8. Repeat until all the beads have been used.

9. Cut the thread to remove the needle and tie the cord ends together, applying a drop of glue to secure the knot.

Floating beads

Different combinations can be used for making floating beads, but the basic principles remain the same. Crimp beads are employed for fixing bead combinations to solid stringing material at certain intervals.

Variations include multistrands or using glue instead of crimp beads for securing the beads to the string. The illustrations show a number of examples. Use the ideas as inspiration for creating a piece that will meet your specific need.

Green and gold
Green floating crystals on gold tigertail will look smart with a formal evening dress or tailored work outfit.

Fit for a bride
The perfect adornment for an evening bride. As the stringing material is barely visible at night, the illusion of "floating" crystals is created.

Ravishing red
Red seed beads and fisheye beads are used for this unusual piece. The two hanging ends, as for a Y chain, distinguish this piece from the rest.

Multistrand floating pearls
With the pearls being glued to the stringing material, this floating multistrand is really quick to make.

Green and gold

This necklace uses green crystals on gold tigertail. Follow the instructions as given for the bridal necklace on page 88, but omit threading the extra lengths of string through the crystals.

Requirements:

- 9 x 8 mm bicone Swarovski crystals (olivine)
- 18 x 4 mm bicone Swarovski crystals (olivine)
- 1 x 6 mm bicone Swarovski crystal (olivine)
- 2 shell ends (brass)
- 1 fastener with extension chain (brass)
- 20 crimp beads (brass)
- 40 cm tigertail (gold)
- Crimping pliers
- Wire cutters

Method:

Follow the instructions on page 88, omitting steps 9–14.

Fit for a bride

This floating neckpiece is the perfect adornment for an evening bride. As the stringing material (tigertail) is barely visible at night, the illusion of "floating" crystals is created. Swarovski crystals are chosen for their splendid luster and light-reflecting quality.

Requirements:

- 9 x 8 mm bicone Swarovski crystals (crystal AB)
- 28 x 4 mm bicone Swarovski crystals (crystal AB)
- 11 x 6 mm bicone Swarovski crystals (crystal AB)
- 2 shell ends (sterling silver)
- 1 fastener with extension chain (sterling silver)
- 40 crimp beads (sterling silver)
- 1 headpin (sterling silver)
- 1 m tigertail
- Crimping pliers
- Wire cutters

Method:

1. Cut a 30 cm length of tigertail for the primary section of the necklace.
2. Following the instructions on page 9, attach a shell end to one end of the tigertail.
3. Attach a crimp bead 2 cm from the shell end.

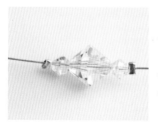

4. Thread a 4 mm crystal, followed by an 8 mm crystal and another 4 mm crystal, onto the string.

5. Thread a crimp bead onto the string and close the crimp bead right up against the group of crystals.
6. Secure the next group of crystals 2.5 cm from the previous group, then repeat until you have nine groups.

7. Attach the remaining shell end 2 cm away, to the other end of the tigertail, as for the beginning.
8. Trim away any excess tigertail.
9. Cut five lengths of tigertail, each 12 cm long.

10. Onto one end of each 12 cm string, thread a crimp bead, followed by a 6 mm crystal, a 4 mm crystal and another crimp bead.

11. Firmly close the crimp beads.

12. Thread the 12 cm strings through the five central 8 mm crystals on the primary section.

13. Repeat steps 10 and 11 for the remaining ends of the 12 cm strings.

14. Now pull the shorter strings until the required effect is obtained when the necklace is worn.
15. Attach the fastener to the ends, then finish off the extension chain with a 6 mm crystal, using a headpin.

Ravishing red

Red seed beads and fisheye beads are used for this unusual piece. The two hanging ends, as for a Y chain, distinguish this floating necklace from the rest.

Requirements:

- 12 x 4 mm fisheye beads (bright red)
- 18 x 11° seed beads (red)
- 22 crimp beads
- 2 shell ends
- 1 fastener
- 50 cm tigertail

Method:

1. Cut the tigertail in two, then attach a shell end to one end of each length (see page 9).
2. Attach a crimp bead 3 cm from each shell end. Attach the fastener to the shell ends.

3. Now thread each string as follows: seed bead, fisheye, seed bead, crimp bead.

4. Firmly close the crimp bead.
5. Secure the next group of beads 3 cm from the previous group, then repeat until each string has four groups.

6. Thread both strings through a crimp bead, followed by a seed bead, fisheye, seed bead and another crimp bead. Firmly close the crimp beads.

7. Thread 3 fisheyes, followed by a crimp bead, onto each string. Find the correct length, then trim away the excess tigertail. Firmly close the crimp beads.

Multistrand with floating pearls

Their subtle gloss and beautiful shapes make pearls the perfect choice for jewelry. Available in countless colors and shapes, each string of pearls possesses its own charm. Every woman should own at least one string of pearls in her lifetime. With the pearls being glued to the stringing material, this floating multistrand is really quick to make. Tigertail works well, but nylon yarn or silk cord is more appropriate for pearls.

Requirements:

- Approximately 40 pearls of various colors and sizes
- 1.5 m tigertail
- 2 cord crimp ends
- 2 jump rings
- 1 fastener
- Quick-drying glue
- Flat-nose pliers

Method:

1. Cut four lengths of tigertail as follows: 30 cm, 35 cm, 40 cm and 45 cm.
2. Insert the ends of all four strings into a cord crimp end, then firmly close the crimp end.
3. Using approximately 10 pearls per string, plan the positioning of the pearls on each string, then mark them with a non-permanent marker.
4. Thread the desired number of pearls onto the first string.
5. Apply quick-drying glue to the mark farthest from the free end, then move one pearl to this position. Hold for a while until it is fairly secure, and repeat for the entire string.
6. Repeat for the remaining three strings.
7. Insert the remaining ends of all four strings into a cord crimp end; close firmly. Connect a jump ring to both ends, then complete the necklace by attaching the fastener.

Earrings

Requiring very few beads and findings, most earrings can be completed in no time. There are countless styles and designs to choose from, all tailorable to every budget and occasion. Swarovski crystals and diamonds are perfect for formal earrings, while inexpensive glass or plastic beads can be employed for more casual styles.

As most of the projects in this chapter simply involve threading beads onto a headpin, which is then connected to an ear wire, only the color of the earrings is given, followed by the type and sequence of the beads used in each case. You will need flat-nose and round-nose pliers for all the projects.

Purple
Swarovski earrings

Pink
Swarovski earrings

Olive
Swarovski earrings

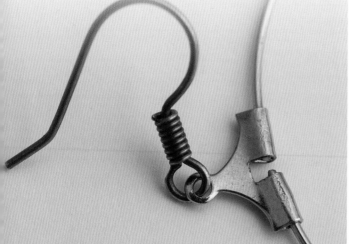

Claret
Swarovski earrings

Pearl and crystal
earrings

Moonstone earrings

Earthy earrings

Olive
chain earrings

Swarovski
hoop earrings

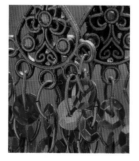

Red sequin earrings

Brown and orange
earrings

Purple Swarovski earrings

1. Thread the following beads onto a headpin:
   - flower spacer
   - 10 mm Swarovski crystal cube (purple)
   - square Swarovski spacer
   - 10 mm Swarovski crystal cube (purple)
2. Make an eyelet above the last crystal, then connect the headpin to the ear wire.
3. Repeat for the second earring.

Pink Swarovski earrings

1. Thread the following beads onto a headpin:
   - 6 mm round Swarovski crystal (dark pink)
   - flower spacer
   - 6 mm bicone Swarovski crystal (light pink)
   - flower spacer
   - 4 mm bicone Swarovski crystal (dark pink)
2. Make an eyelet above the last crystal, then connect the headpin to the ear wire.
3. Repeat for the second earring.

Olive-green Swarovski earrings

(These earrings match the magnetic bracelet on page 60)

1. Thread the following beads onto a headpin:
   • 3 mm spacer (brass)
   • 4 mm round Swarovski crystal (olivine)
   • 3 mm spacer (brass)
   • 4 mm round Swarovski crystal (olivine)
   • 3 mm spacer (brass)
   • 4 mm bicone Swarovski crystal (olivine)
2. Make an eyelet above the last crystal, then connect the headpin to the ear wire.
3. Repeat for the second earring.

Claret Swarovski earrings

(These earrings match the multistrand necklace on page 136)

1. Thread the following beads onto a headpin:
   • flower spacer
   • 6 mm flat round Swarovski crystal (light siam)
   • flower spacer
   • 6 mm bicone Swarovski crystal (light siam)
   • flower spacer
   • 4 mm round Swarovski crystal (light siam)
   • flower spacer
   • 4 mm bicone Swarovski crystal (light siam)
2. Make an eyelet above the last crystal, then connect the headpin to the ear wire.
3. Repeat for the second earring.

Pearl and crystal earrings

(These earrings match the necklace on page 76)

1. Thread the following beads onto a headpin:
   - flower spacer
   - 6 mm pearl
   - flower spacer
   - 6 mm bicone Swarovski crystal (golden shadow)
   - flower spacer
   - 6 mm pearl
   - flower spacer
   - 4 mm bicone Swarovski crystal (golden shadow)
2. Make an eyelet above the last crystal, then connect the headpin to the ear wire.
3. Repeat for the second earring.

Earthy earrings

(These earrings match the multistrand necklace on page 128)

1. Thread the following beads onto a headpin:
   - mother-of-pearl smartie bead (brown)
   - 8° seed bead (brown)
   - 6 mm round faceted glass bead (brown)
   - 4 mm fire-polished glass bead (olive green)
   - 3 mm oval wooden bead
   - 11° seed bead (matte brown)
2. Make an eyelet above the last bead, then connect the headpin to the ear wire.
3. Repeat for the second earring.

Swarovski hoop earrings

(These earrings match the multistrand crystal
bracelet on page 44)

Requirements:

- 10 x 6 mm round Swarovski crystals (topaz)
- 6 x 6 mm round Swarovski crystals (golden shadow)
- 4 x 6 mm bicone Swarovski crystals (olivine)
- 4 x 6 mm bicone Swarovski crystals (golden shadow)
- 2 x 4 mm round Swarovski crystals (golden shadow)
- 18 x 4 mm bicone Swarovski crystals (olivine)
- 10 Chinese crystals (olive green)
- 6 x 6 mm pearls (champagne)
- 10 headpins (brass)
- 38 eyepins (brass)
- 2 hoop earrings (brass)
- 2 ear wires (brass)
- Round-nose pliers
- Flat-nose pliers

Method:

Use headpins and eyepins to link the crystals when making
the strings for steps 1–3.

1. Thread a pearl, Chinese crystal, 6 mm round crystal (topaz),
   Chinese crystal — make four strings.
2. Thread a 6 mm round crystal (golden shadow), 6 mm bicone crystal (olivine), 6 mm round crystal (topaz), 4 mm bicone crystal (olivine), 6 mm bicone crystal (golden shadow)
   — make four strings.
3. Thread a 6 mm round crystal (golden shadow), 4 mm bicone
   crystal (olivine), 6 mm round crystal (topaz), Chinese crystal, 4
   mm round crystal (golden shadow), pearl — make two strings.
4. Thread the strings onto the hoop as follows, alternating with 4
   mm bicone Swarovski crystals: crystal, string 1, crystal, string 2,
   crystal, string 3, crystal, string 2, crystal, string 1, crystal.
5. Slip the end of the hoop into the opening, then firmly pinch
   the hoop closed.
6. Connect the ear wire to the hoop.
7. Repeat steps 2–4 for the second earring.

Chain earrings

The same basic method is applied for the following three pairs of earrings, connecting different lengths of chain to a focal bead or ear wire.

Brown and orange earrings

Requirements:

- 6 headpins (brass)
- 2 focal beads (brass)
- 4 x 6 mm bicone Swarovski crystals (orange)
- 4 x 6 mm bicone Swarovski crystals (crystal AB)
- 2 x 4 mm bicone Swarovski crystals (orange)
- 2 ear wires (brass)
- 8 flower spacers (brass)
- 4 x 3 mm spacers (brass)
- 14 cm chain (brass)
- Round-nose pliers
- Flat-nose pliers
- Wire cutters

Method:

1. Make three different strings as follows:

   a. Thread a 6 mm orange crystal onto a headpin, then make an eyelet. Connect to 3.5 cm of chain.
   b. Thread a 6 mm orange crystal onto a headpin, then make an eyelet. Connect to 3 cm of chain.
   c. Thread a 3 mm spacer, followed by a 6 mm crystal AB, flower spacer, 4 mm orange crystal, flower spacer, 6 mm crystal AB and another 3 mm spacer, onto a headpin, then make an eyelet.
2. Thread a flower spacer, followed by a focal bead and another flower spacer, onto an eyepin, then make a second eyelet on the opposite side.
3. Connect the three strings to the bottom of the focal bead and an ear wire to the top.

4. Repeat for the second earring.

Moonstone earrings

(These earrings match the moonstone
necklace on page 132)

Requirements:

- 2 spiral charms (silver)
- 4 small moonstone cubes
- 2 oval moonstone beads, top-drilled
- 2 heart-lock charms (silver)
- 2 jump rings (silver)
- 6 short headpins (silver)
- 10 cm fine chain (silver)
- 2 ear wires (silver)

Method:

1. Cut two 2.5 cm and two 1.5 cm lengths of chain.
2. Thread each moonstone cube and spiral charm onto a separate headpin, then make an eyelet for each.
3. Connect a jump ring to each moonstone oval.
4. Connect the different components to the chains as illustrated.
5. Connect the chains to the ear wires.
6. Repeat for the second earring.

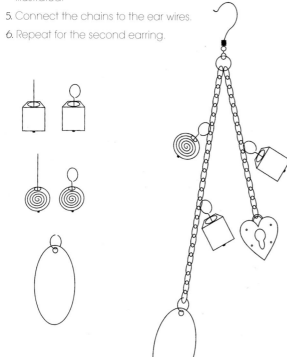

Olive-green chain earrings

(These earrings match the floating necklace on page 87)

Requirements:

- 2 oval jump rings
- 2 x 8 mm bicone Swarovski crystals (olivine)
- 4 x 6 mm bicone Swarovski crystals (olivine)
- 4 x 4 mm bicone Swarovski crystals (olivine)
- 2 x 4 mm round Swarovski crystals (olivine)
- 12 short headpins (brass)
- 2 ear wires
- 16 cm fine chain (brass)

Method:

1. Cut two 3.5 cm, two 2.5 cm and two 2 cm lengths of chain.
2. Thread each crystal onto a separate headpin, then make an eyelet for each.
3. Connect each oval jump ring to an ear wire, then insert the chains into the jump rings.
4. Connect the crystals to the chains as illustrated.
5. Repeat for the second earring.

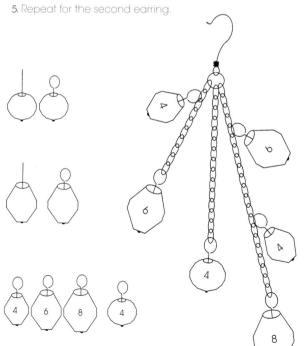

Red sequin earrings

Requirements:

- 2 eardrops with 5 eyelets (brass)
- 2 ear wires (brass)
- 58 thin oval jump rings (brass)
- 116 red sequins
- 6 small red gemstones
- Flat-nose pliers
- Quick-drying glue

Method:

1. Insert two sequins into a jump ring, then bend the ring closed.

2. Insert two more sequins into another jump ring, then link the second ring to the first between the first two sequins.

3. Repeat until you have four strings of five jump rings, four strings of six and two strings of seven.

4. Connect the sequined jump rings to the eardrops, with the longest string in the middle and the shorter strings toward the sides.

5. Glue the small red gemstones to the eardrops.

6. Attach the ear wires.

7. Repeat for the second earring.

Twine, cord and ribbon

Sometimes all you need for creating an extraordinary piece of jewelry is to attach a pretty pendant to a simple cord or ribbon.

Decorative cord, combined with a few beads, can also become a focal point. Special twines and cords require fewer beads, making for more • affordable jewelry.

Heart with thongs and ribbon

An exquisite metal heart with gemstones on the one side and beautiful patterns on the other side.

Roped mother-of-pearl

A beautiful pendant requiring only a suitable cord to turn it into an exceptional piece of jewelry.

Macramé lariat

This works exceptionally well if you use thin black twine combined with Swarovski crystals and silver beads.

Silver twine necklace

I loved this thin silver twine and did not want it covered in too many beads. Embellishing the ends only was a perfect solution.

Heart with thongs and ribbon

This exquisite metal heart, with gemstones on the one side and pretty patterns on the other, is an excellent example of a component that needs nothing more than thongs and ribbon to create a stunning piece of jewelry. The thongs are genuine leather in rich metallic colors, softened by a narrow organza ribbon in champagne. The heart can be worn any way around.

Requirements:

- 1 fancy heart pendant (brass)
- 50 cm each of thin leather thong in copper, brass and olive green
- 50 cm x 3 mm organza ribbon (champagne)
- 2 cord crimp ends (brass)
- 1 trigger clasp (brass)
- 2 jump rings (brass)
- Flat-nose pliers

Method:

1. Cut all the thongs and ribbon to the exact same length, then join them together using a cord crimp end on either end.
2. Thread the thongs and ribbon through the pendant loop.
3. Attach the jump rings and fastener.

Roped mother-of-pearl

Another beautiful pendant requiring only a cord to create a special piece of jewelry. To complement the colors in the pendant, seed-bead strings, cord and ball-link chain are braided together to make a fancy rope.

Requirements:

- 1 round pendant with shell inlays
- 1 m beading cord (blue)
- 1 m ball-link chain
- 1 g 11° Japanese seed beads (purple pink)
- 1 g 11° Japanese seed beads (blue green)
- 2 m thin nylon yarn
- 1 bail (silver)
- 2 cones (antique silver)
- 2 shell ends (silver)
- 1 jump ring (silver)
- 1 trigger clasp (silver)
- Beading needle
- Flat-nose pliers

Method:

1. Connect the bail to the pendant.

2. Cut the nylon yarn into two 1 m lengths, then thread the purple-pink seed beads onto one length and the blue-green seed beads onto the other.

3. Stick masking tape to the ends of the strings to prevent the beads from slipping off.

4. Hold one end of the seed-bead strings, beading cord and chain together using a spring bead stopper.

5. Braid the two seed-bead strings, beading cord and chain together, treating the cord and chain as one string.

6. Once you are happy with the length, thread the braid through the bail on the pendant.

7. Finish the ends as follows: Wrap nymo yarn around the ends to secure them tightly. Thread the yarn through a cone, then attach a shell end following the instructions on page 9.

8. Repeat for the remaining end.

9. Attach the jump ring and fastener.

Macramé lariat

Macramé braiding, although sometimes called Chinese knotting, did not originate in China as the name might suggest, but in 13th-century Arabia. The art was passed on from generation to generation by sailors who, during their endless voyages, made decorative items out of sisal rope, which were then traded at harbors where they stopped. It was these sailors who taught the Chinese the art of macramé.

Macramé comprises a large variety of knots, which are not discussed in detail in this book. Only two basic knots are used for the lariat illustrated here.

Thin cords in different shades of blue show up the knots clearly. For a striking variation, use black cord embellished with silver beads or Swarovski crystals. Or choose decorative silver, gold or multicolored metallic yarn combined with plain beads — the fancier the cord, the less prominent the beads should be.

Half knot

1. Start with four lengths of cord. The two light-blue inner cords, known as the core cords, are left hanging in the center, while the two dark-blue outer cords are knotted around them.
2. Take the left-hand outer cord over the core cords and under the right-hand outer cord.
3. Take the right-hand outer cord under the core cords and through the loop formed by the left-hand outer cord.
4. Pull the cords tight.
5. Repetition of this knot results in a spiral.

Flat knot

Start by making a half knot as described on page 110. The second half of the knot is the opposite of the first half, taking the right-hand outer cord over the core cords and under the left-hand outer cord. Now take the left-hand outer cord under the core cords and through the loop. Pull the cords tight. Repeating this knot results in a flat, wide braid.

Requirements:

- 8 m beading cord (4 m light blue, 4 m dark blue)
- 1 large focal bead (blue and brown)
- 2 smaller focal beads (blue)
- 9 x 6 mm fisheye beads (blue)
- 1 x 10 mm fisheye bead (blue)
- 3 x 6 mm bicone Swarovski crystals (2 blue, 1 brown)
- 2 x 8 mm fisheye beads (brown)
- 1 x 4 mm fisheye bead (brown)
- 2 x 6 mm tubular fisheye beads (brown)
- 2 cord crimp ends
- 1 jump ring
- 1 trigger clasp
- Clear nail polish
- Flat-nose pliers

Method:

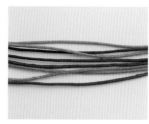

1. Cut the beading cord into eight 1 m lengths.

2. Thread all eight strings through the large focal bead.

3. Thread a different bead onto the end of each of the eight strings, then tie a secure knot in each end.

4. Apply clear nail polish to each knot to prevent it from coming undone.

5. Divide the eight strings into two groups of four, then tie a single knot above the focal bead.

6. Make 10 flat knots in each of the two four-cord strings. For added interest, use the light-blue cords as core cord on one side, and the dark-blue cords as core cord on the other side.

7. Thread all four strings through the smaller focal bead on either side. Switching the colors of the core cords, make 10 more flat knots on either side.

8. Thread a 6 mm fisheye bead onto each of the four outer cords, then make 10 more flat knots on either side.

9. Thread a brown tubular fisheye bead onto the core cords on either side.

10. Switching the colors of the core cords, make 20 half knots to form a spiral.

11. Repeat on the other side.

12. Thread a 6 mm fisheye bead onto each of the four core cords, then tie all four strings together just above the beads.

13. Repeat on the other side.

14. Insert the ends of all four strings into a cord crimp end on either side, then firmly close the crimp end.

15. Attach the jump ring to one end and the fastener to the other.

Silver twine necklace

The pretty silver twine needs very little embellishment to make a striking necklace.

Requirements:

- 10 m silver twine
- 38 x 6 mm round fisheye beads (white)
- 2 cord crimp ends
- 1 trigger clasp
- Flat-nose pliers
- Quick-drying glue

Method:

1. Cut 20 x 50 cm strings of twine.

2. Tie the strings together 12 cm from one end.

3. Trim the ends below the knot to different lengths.

4. Randomly thread fisheye beads onto the string ends, limiting each string to three beads. Tie a knot in the end of each string to prevent the beads from slipping off.

5. Glue the beads to the strings in several different positions.

6. Allow the glue to dry completely, then divide the strings above the knot into two groups.

7. Insert the ends of each group into a cord crimp end, firmly close the crimp end and attach the fastener.

Timeless elegance

Gone are the days when the only purpose of a wristwatch was to tell the time! Today a watch is a piece of jewelry to complement an outfit, often exchanged daily by the wearer.

Watch faces can be bought fairly cheaply, and, depending on the beads you use, you can easily make one for every day of the week. A handmade watch bracelet also makes a great gift, which will no doubt be deeply appreciated by a special person in your life. If you are in doubt as to which color will be liked best, adorn the fob with metal charms.

Vintage rose watch
The clay roses and brown pearls are a perfect match for the copper watch face, giving the piece a vintage feel.

Pearls and seed beads
An unusual combination of glass pearls and seed beads makes for a special watch.

Crystal bracelet watches
With the vast variety of crystal colors on the market, the possibilities for creating exquisite wristbands are endless.

White chain watch
The watch face differs from other watch faces in that only one side is connected to a chain or string.

Vintage rose watch

The clay roses and brown pearls are a perfect match for the copper watch face, giving the piece a vintage feel.

Requirements:

- 1 watch face (copper)
- 8 clay roses (2 each in 4 different colors)
- 20 x 4 mm pearls (brown)
- 72 x 8° seed beads (brown)
- 2 shell ends (copper)
- 2 crimp beads (copper)
- 2 jump rings (copper)
- 1 trigger clasp (copper)
- 80 cm stringing material (tigertail or nylon yarn)
- Flat-nose pliers
- Crimping pliers

Method:

1. Cut the stringing material in two, then thread one string through the opening of the watch face, doubling up the string.
2. Thread the pearls, seed beads and roses onto the strings as follows: 1 pearl, 2 seed beads onto each string separately; both strings through first clay rose; 2 seed beads, 1 pearl, 2 seed beads onto each string separately; both strings through second clay rose.
3. Repeat the sequence two more times, ending with 2 seed beads, 1 pearl, 2 seed beads onto each string separately.
4. Thread both strings through a shell end, then finish off using a crimp bead (see page 9).
5. Repeat for the other side of the watch, then attach the jump rings and fastener.

Step 1

Step 2

Step 2

Pearls and seed beads

An unusual combination of glass pearls and seed beads makes for a special watch.

Requirements:

- 1 watch face (antique silver)
- 10 x 10 mm glass pearls (medium gray)
- Approximately 200 x 11° seed beads (silver white)
- 2 shell ends
- 80 cm stringing material
  (tigertail or nylon yarn)
- 1 toggle clasp
- 2 beading needles
- Flat-nose pliers
- Crimping pliers

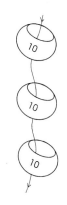

Second Needle

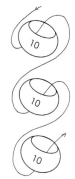

First Needle

Method:

1. Cut the stringing material in two, then thread one string through the opening of the watch face, doubling up the string.

2. Thread one end of the string through the eye of a beading needle, then pick up nine seed beads.

3. Thread the needle through a pearl, starting from the bottom end of the pearl.

4. Pick up 19 seed beads, then thread the needle through the next pearl, starting from the bottom.

5. Thread the remaining end of the string through the eye of the second beading needle.

6. Thread the second needle through the first pearl, starting from the top end of the pearl, then through the 10th bead of the group of 19 seed beads (see diagram).

7. Repeat steps 4–6 three more times, ending with the seed bead threaded onto both strings.

8. Pick up nine seed beads onto the first needle.

9. Thread the second needle through the last pearl, starting from the top end of the pearl, then through the last seed bead on the first string.

10. Finish off with a shell end threaded onto both strings simultaneously (see page 9).

11. Repeat for the other side of the watch, then attach the toggle clasp.

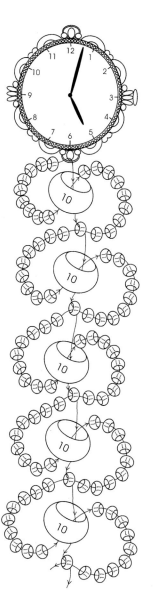

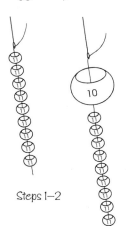

Steps 1—2

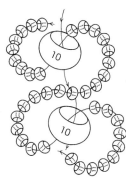

Step 6

Crystal bracelet watches

Swarovski crystals and sliders make a fabulous combination. With the vast variety of colors on the market, the possibilities for creating exquisite wristbands are endless.

Requirements:

- 1 watch face
- 16 x 4 mm bicone Swarovski crystals (color 1)
- 16 x 4 mm bicone Swarovski crystals (color 2)
- 6 Swarovski sliders (4 of the same, 2 different)
- 50 cm tigertail
- 1 wrap clasp
- 2 crimp beads
- Crimping pliers
- Flat-nose pliers

Method:

1. Cut the tigertail in two, then thread one string through the opening of the watch face, doubling up the string.

2. Thread the Swarovski crystals onto the two strings as follows: first string: color 1, color 2; second string: color 2, color 1.

3. Thread a Swarovski slider onto both strings simultaneously.

4. Repeat steps 2 and 3 two more times, then step 2 once more.

5. End with a slider and repeat for the other side of the watch. For a longer strap, add more crystals and end with a crimp bead.

6. Attach the clasp.

White chain watch

This watch face differs from other watch faces in that only one side can be connected to a foundation chain or string. Use it as a pendant, or attached to a charm bracelet as shown here. The bracelet is further embellished with beads, metal flowers and silver balls.

Requirements:

- 18–20 cm bracelet chain with toggle clasp (silver)
- 1 watch face (white and silver)
- Variety of white beads, silver metal flowers and flower trinkets
- Flower spacers (silver)
- Headpins (silver)
- 17 jump rings

Method:

1. Connect the watch face to the center of the chain using a jump ring.

2. Using the photographs as inspiration, link the beads and metal trimmings into clusters, then connect them to the chain using jump rings.

Multistrand necklaces

Creating multistrands probably gives me greater pleasure than any other type of beadwork! They are versatile, and with simple color and bead variations special and unique pieces are produced time after time. During the planning stage, special attention should be given to color combinations, making for diverse types of jewelry.

Split stranding is a variation of multistranding where some of the beads are threaded onto more than one string before splitting them again to be strung separately.

Bountiful brown
This is a classic example of combining various types of beads and an interesting chain.

Double string in soft green and pink
The variety and shapes of the green and pink beads make an interesting combination.

Moonstone and chains
Moonstone has a special charm, its color ranging from a tinge of blue white to a tawny glimmer, taking on the hue of nearby colors.

Girly multistrand with roses
Organza bows and clay beads adorn this multistrand in shades of orange.

Combination multistrand

A quick and easy piece that can be considered a combination of floating beads and multistranding.

Indian charm

Split stranding is used as a variation of multistranding, resulting in interesting cluster formations.

Black split strand with large drop pendant

A string of classic black pearls worn with it accentuates the beauty of this elegant split strand.

Multistrand choker

Here, Japanese seed beads are combined with freshwater pearls, gemstone chips and flower-shaped glass beads.

Bountiful brown

This is a classic example of combining various types of beads and an interesting chain. Diverse beads can sometimes be risky, but in this case they are highly effective. The necklace consists of six strings, all different from one another.

Requirements:

- 11 mother-of-pearl smartie beads (brown)
- 11 x 6 mm faceted glass beads (brown)
- 2 g x 11° seed beads (purple pink)
- 2 g x 11° seed beads (metallic luster)
- 2 g x 8° seed beads (brown)
- 90–100 x 5 mm fire-polished glass beads (olive green)
- 60 x 4 mm oval wooden beads
- 20 wooden spacers
- 38 cm decorative chain (copper)
- 2 cord crimp ends (copper)
- 2 jump rings
- 1 fastener with extension chain (copper)
- Nymo yarn, size D
- Flat-nose pliers
- Beading needle

Method:

1. Thread the needle and pick up beads as indicated. All the strings are approximately 38 cm in length.

2. First string: purple-pink seed beads; second string: fire-polished glass beads.

3. Third string: 10 metallic-luster seed beads, 1 smartie bead — repeat 10 more times.

4. Fourth string: 10 brown seed beads, 1 x 6 mm glass bead — repeat 10 more times.

5. Fifth string: 3 wooden oval beads, 1 wooden spacer — repeat 19 more times.
6. Sixth string: decorative chain.

7. Following the instructions on page 10, insert the ends of all six strings into a cord crimp end on either end of the necklace.
8. Connect a jump ring to both ends, then complete the necklace by attaching the fastener.

Double string in soft green and pink

The variety of bead shapes in this necklace lends interest to the piece. Although only glass beads are used here, they will make a striking combination alternated with pearls.

Requirements:

- 32 faceted glass drops (bright green)
- 16 flat rectangular glass beads (pale green)
- 32 x 2 mm silver beads
- 58 pressed glass drops (pink)
- 84 pressed glass crescents (crystal)
- 1 m tigertail
- Magnetic clasp
- 4 crimp beads
- Multistrand connector
- Round-nose pliers
- Flat-nose pliers

Method:

Both strings are threaded in the same sequence, starting at different points with the inner string shorter than the outer.

1. Thread the inner string as follows: 1 silver bead, 2 green drops, 1 silver bead, 3 crystal crescents, 2 pink drops, 1 flat rectangular bead, 2 pink drops, 3 crystal crescents. Repeat five more times, then end the string with 1 silver bead, followed by 2 green drops and 1 silver bead.

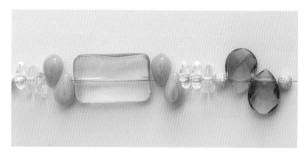

2. Thread the outer string in the same order, starting with 2 pink drops. Repeat step 1 sequence six times; end the string with 2 pink drops, a flat rectangular bead and 2 pink drops.

3. Pull both strings fairly tight, ensuring that the green and pink drops lie in opposite directions.

4. Thread both ends of each string through a crimp bead, then through one hole of the multistrand connector and back through the crimp bead again. Firmly close the crimp beads, then thread the strings back through at least five beads.

5. Attach the two sections of the magnetic clasp to the ends.

Moonstone and chains

Although this necklace takes a little longer to make, it is still very easy and definitely worth your while. Moonstone has a special charm, its color ranging from a tinge of blue white to a tawny glimmer, taking on the hue of nearby colors. It looks exceptionally pretty worn with blue. There are instructions for matching earrings on page 102.

Requirements:

- 4 x 35 mm flat oval moonstone beads
- 2 x 15 mm flat oval faceted moonstone beads
- 16 x 4 mm round moonstone beads
- 2 small oval moonstone beads, top-drilled
- 6 x 2 mm round moonstone beads
- 6 x 6 mm flat round moonstone beads
- 2 flower-shaped glass beads
- 2 x 2 mm silver beads
- 2 x 4 mm silver filigree beads

The following in silver base metal:

- 8 flower spacers
- 5 x 12 mm jump rings
- 19 x 7 mm jump rings
- 4 x 5 mm jump rings
- 9 long eyepins
- 20 short headpins
- 1 bead cap to fit faceted oval bead
- 1 m fine silver chain
- 1 fastener

- Round-nose pliers
- Flat-nose pliers
- Wire cutters

Method:

1. Cut the chain into two 14 cm lengths and four 18 cm lengths.
2. Thread each 35 mm bead onto an eyepin, then make a second eyelet on the opposite side of the bead.

3. Using the 12 mm jump rings, link the four large beads together, then connect the remaining large jump rings to either end of the string.

4. Connect the two 14 cm chains to the jump rings on either end, then connect two of the 18 cm chains to the same jump rings.

5. With photographs as guide, make beaded charms. Connect to the 7 mm jump rings. Combine in clusters and connect to large jump rings between large moonstones.

6. For the shorter inner string, thread groups of beads onto eyepins as follows, then make a second eyelet on the opposite side of the group so that you have one eyelet on either side of each group:

   a. 2 mm round moonstone bead, 4 mm round moonstone bead, 2 mm round moonstone bead — make two.

   b. 6 mm flat round moonstone bead, 4 mm round moonstone bead — make two.

   c. 2 mm round moonstone bead, 15 mm flat oval moonstone bead, 2 mm round moonstone bead — make one.

7. Using the 5 mm jump rings, link these combinations as follows: a, b, c, b, a.

8. Using a 7 mm jump ring, connect the remaining two 18 cm chains to either end of this string.

9. Connect one 7 mm jump ring to the 18 cm chains at either end of each string, so that each jump ring contains two 18 cm chains. Attach the fastener.

Girly multistrand with roses

Organza bows and clay beads adorn this multistrand in shades of orange. With each of the three strings comprising only one type of bead, it is quick and easy to make. Once threaded, the ends are finished off with brown bead caps. Two or three seed beads at each end will help the bead caps fit snugly.

Requirements:

- 70 x 7 mm fire-polished glass beads (orange)
- 100 x 5 mm fire-polished glass beads (honey)
- 1 g x 3 mm bugle beads (matte apricot)
- 2 bead caps (copper)
- 2 shell ends (copper)
- 2 crimp beads (copper)
- 2 clay roses (pale orange)
- 20 cm organza ribbon (bright orange)
- 1 trigger clasp
- 2 jump rings (copper)
- Nymo yarn, size D
- Beading needle
- Flat-nose pliers
- Crimping pliers

Method:

1. Thread the needle with the nymo yarn, then make three bead strings as shown, beginning and ending each string with two or three seed beads. Make the bugle string 47 cm long.

2. Thread all three strings through a bead cap, then attach a shell end (see page 9).

3. Repeat for the remaining end.
4. Attach the jump rings and fastener.

5. Tie an organza bow around all three strings, approximately 15 cm from the fastener on either end.

6. Using a needle and nymo yarn, sew a clay rose to the center of each bow.

Multistrand combination necklace

This quick and easy piece can be considered a combination of floating beads and multistranding. Only fisheye beads are used here, but other combinations such as pearls and gemstone chips, or Swarovski crystals in different shapes and sizes, will also work well. The same technique is followed for the necklace below left, replacing the tigertail with 10 fine nylon yarns and alternating various shapes and sizes of Swarovski and Chinese crystals, all in claret. Although this takes a little longer to complete, it is still very easy.

Requirements:

- 4 x 15 mm round fisheye beads (pink)
- 5 x 10 mm oval fisheye beads (pink)
- 7 x 8 mm round fisheye beads (beige)
- 7 x 6 mm round fisheye beads (white)
- 12 x 4 mm round fisheye beads (brown)
- 3.5 m tigertail
- 2 cord crimp ends
- 2 jump rings
- 1 trigger clasp
- Crimping pliers
- Flat-nose pliers
- Wire cutters

Method:

1. Cut the tigertail into seven lengths of 50 cm each.

2. Insert the ends of all seven strings into a cord crimp end, then firmly close the crimp end.

3. Using the photographs as inspiration, randomly thread the beads onto the seven strings in different combinations.

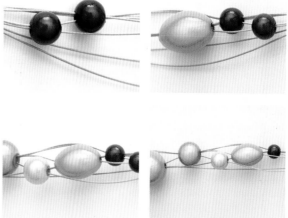

4. When all the beads have been used, finish the remaining ends of the strings using a cord crimp end, then attach the jump rings and trigger clasp.

Indian charm

In this project a variation of multistranding called split-stranding is used. Some beads are threaded onto separate strings and others onto both, with the Bali-silver spacers and beads lending an Indian air. Although only fisheyes are used here, other glass beads or Swarovski crystals will be equally effective. The recommended cord has a wax coating for ease of stringing.

Requirements:

- 12 x 8 mm fisheye beads (brown)
- 12 x 8 mm fisheye beads (orange)
- 11 x 8 mm fisheye beads (beige)
- 24 x 4 mm fisheye beads (brown)
- 24 x 4 mm fisheye beads (orange)
- 22 x 4 mm fisheye beads (beige)
- 17 x 6 mm oval Bali-silver beads
- 36 x 3 mm Bali-silver spacers
- 1 trigger clasp
- 1 m waxed beading cord
- 2 jump rings
- Flat-nose pliers

Method:

1. Following the instructions on page 10, attach a jump ring to the cord.

2. Thread both strings through a Bali-silver spacer, a Bali-silver bead and another spacer.

3. Split the strings, thread the fisheyes onto the two separate strings as follows: string 1: 4 mm, 8 mm, 4 mm beige; string 2: 4 mm, 8 mm, 4 mm orange.

4. Thread both strings through a Bali-silver spacer, a Bali-silver bead and another spacer.

5. Splitting the strings again, thread fisheyes onto the separate strings as in step 3, using brown for the first string and beige for the second string.

6. Thread both strings through a spacer, bead and another spacer, then thread fisheyes (orange for the first string and brown for the second).

7. Thread both strings through a Bali-silver spacer, a Bali-silver bead and another spacer.
8. Repeat steps 3–8 until the required length is reached, ending with a Bali-silver spacer.
9. Thread both strings through the remaining jump ring and back through the spacer. Knot and thread through several beads to strengthen.

Black split strand with large drop pendant

A string of classic black pearls accentuates the beauty of this elegant split strand. The technique used here can be applied in different ways using a variety of beads.

Requirements:

Use shiny black beads throughout:

- 10 x 6 mm round glass beads
- 11 x 10 mm faceted round beads
- 10 x 8 mm flat round glass beads
- 75 cm beading cord (black)
- 1 large faceted drop pendant
- 1 bail (sterling silver)
- 2 cord crimp ends (sterling silver)
- 1 toggle clasp (sterling silver)
- 2 jump rings (sterling silver)
- Flat-nose pliers

Method:

1. Cut the length of beading cord in two.
2. Connect the bail to the drop pendant.
3. Insert the ends of both strings into a cord crimp end, then firmly close the crimp end.

4. Thread both strings through five 6 mm round beads.

5. Split the strings and ensure you know which is string 1 and which is string 2.

6. Thread the beads as follows: faceted round bead string 1 only, flat round bead both strings, faceted round bead string 2 only, flat round bead both strings.

7. Repeat until you have threaded five faceted beads.

8. Thread the sixth faceted bead onto string 2, followed by the drop pendant onto string 1 and a flat round bead onto both strings.

9. Repeat step 6 using all the faceted beads.
10. Thread both strings through five 6 mm round beads, and finish the ends of the strings using a cord crimp end.

11. Attach the jump rings and toggle clasp.

Multistrand choker

This pretty choker is very easy to make. By using different beads and colors, a variety of unique pieces can be created. Here, Japanese seed beads are combined with freshwater pearls, gemstone chips and flower-shaped glass beads. Clay roses on a brass choker or brown seed beads with pearls will also make stunning combinations.

Requirements:

- 1 solid choker
- 2 m fine metal wire
- Japanese seed beads (silver white)
- Variety of colored rice pearls
- Variety of gemstone chips
- 3 flower-shaped glass beads
- 3 headpins
- Wire cutters

Method:

1. Cut the metal wire into two 1 m lengths.

2. Thread seed beads onto one length of wire, leaving 1.5 cm clear at either end. Wind the string around the choker, tightly securing the ends.

3. Randomly thread the colored rice pearls and gemstone chips onto the remaining length of wire, leaving 1.5 cm clear at either end. Wind the string around the choker as before.

4. Using the headpins, connect the three flower-shaped beads to the choker (center and sides).

Author's acknowledgments

To Paul and my children, thank you for your patience once again while I neglected the household to complete the book. Thank you for encouraging me when I felt like giving up.

To Jaco and Nicolette, thank you for all your designs and clever ideas. Thank you to Corlé and Francia for your advice and honest opinions when the designs I came up with did not tickle your fancy. Thank you also for your help with making the jewelry and for your sympathy when I had to work late into the night.

To Settie Malherbe, thank you for your interest and help, and for allowing me to include some of your designs in the book. The Silver heart chain (page 26), Copper charms (page 32), Pink and brown bracelet (page 54) and the Blue cluster bracelet (page 56) were designed and made by Settie.

To Wilsia, thank you so much for your support and patience! I have no doubt that there were times when you wanted to do something drastic, but then you just tactfully tightened the screws on me.

Thank you to Ivan Naudé for the professional and serene way in which you took the photographs. You truly are an artist without any airs or whims.

Thanks, Angie, for the lovely layout which shows off the jewelry to its best advantage, and thank you Louise for the excellent translation and your meticulous eye for detail.

Above all, thank you to my heavenly Father for giving me the strength to complete this project.

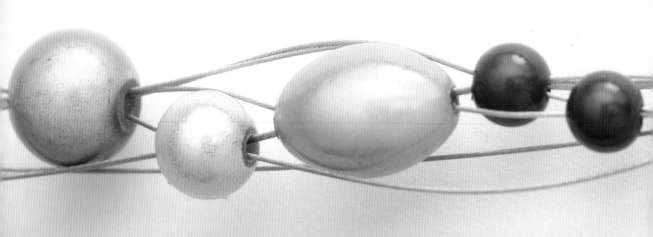